Clan Forbes

Official Guide

Published independently through Amazon Kindle Direct Publishing.

Cover design by B.R. Forbes

For information about this book:
Clan Forbes Society
Saltgrass Avenue, Surfside Beach, Texas 77541

For more information regarding the content,
please visit the website at www.Clan-Forbes.org

Clan Forbes Society, Inc., is a charitable, cultural and educational organization dedicated to helping and encouraging all those with lineage from the Scottish House of Forbes to connect with their Scottish heritage by presenting historical research and creating of a sense of community. Membership is open to all individuals, regardless of their surname or lineage.

ISBN: 979-8-9908530-2-7

My own personal view is that anyone – whatever their current name – who regards themselves as in any way associated with the clan should be welcomed with open arms!

As you can imagine, we receive a lot of visits from people claiming to have connections, including of course some on the "official" list of septs, and I always try to encourage them to wear the tartan.

In this troubled world, I think there is every reason for encouragement to be given to anyone who would like to be associated to our peaceful clan where grace is our guide.

FORBES
Malcolm, 23rd Lord Forbes
Castle Forbes, Aberdeenshire, Scotland

Preface: Purpose of This Guide

For more than eight centuries, the name Forbes has been woven into the history of Scotland—its landscapes, its conflicts, its triumphs, and its enduring cultural traditions. From the Gaelic settlements in Aberdeenshire to the global communities of Forbes descendants today, the story of the clan is one of resilience, service, and a steadfast commitment to heritage. This guide honors that legacy and provides members, families, and friends with a clear, accurate, and engaging resource that reflects the true history and identity of Clan Forbes.

This comprehensive, authoritative guide brings together our origins, our cadet branches, our castles and estates, our notable figures, and the traditions that continue to bind us as a global community. This work is the result of years of research, collaboration, and dedication to historical integrity. It is designed not only as a reference, but as an invitation: an invitation to explore, to learn, and to take pride in the remarkable story of our people.

It is important to note that several unofficial "clan guides" and commercial booklets circulate online and at events, often produced without consultation, verification, or involvement from the Clan Forbes Society. While some contain fragments of accurate information, they are not the work of the Society, nor do they reflect the depth of research, cultural stewardship, or historical responsibility that this official guide represents. This publication is the only guide developed, reviewed, and endorsed by the Clan Forbes Society, which receives all net proceeds from the sale of this book.

In these pages, you will encounter the landscapes that shaped our ancestors, the leaders who guided our clan through turbulent centuries, the traditions that continue to define us, and the global diaspora that carries the Forbes name into the future. Whether you are a lifelong member, a newly discovered descendant, or simply a friend of the clan, we hope this guide deepens your connection to our shared heritage.

Grace me guide.

Table of Contents

Part I — Clan Forbes

Part II — Brief History

Part III — Heritage Sites

Part IV — Beyond Scotland

Part V — Achievement

Part VI — Clan Forbes Society

Part I – Clan Forbes

Ochonochar Forbhasach

The story of Clan Forbes begins with the Gaelic warrior Ochonochar, whose legend emerged during the clashes between the ancient kingdoms of the Picts and Dalreudini in the region now called Aberdeenshire.

The Picts were Iron Age Britons who were driven north by the Romans to what we now call Scotland. The name "Picti" likely derived from the Latin meaning "painted people," a reference to their reputed use of tattoos or body paint. They called themselves "firu Fortrenn"—the men of Fortriu. Pictland comprised seven provinces: Cait, Cé, Circin, Fib, Fidach, Fotla, and Fortriu, each attributed to a son of the legendary founder Cruithne. Cé, the land of the first son, corresponds to modern-day Aberdeenshire.

Pictish dominance in the region was challenged by invaders from the west. In the fifth century, the legendary chieftain Reuda (or Riada) led Irish Gaels—known in Latin as Scotti—from northeastern Ireland across the North Channel to settle on Scotland's western coast. The Gaels established settlements on the western islands and coastline. Their territory became known as Dál Riada, meaning "Riada's share or portion," and the people were called the Dalreudini. Their early settlements were overwhelmed by the native Picts, but they pushed farther east, waging battles between 558 CE and 767 CE.

In the late ninth century, the Pictish kingdom merged with Dál Riata to form the Kingdom of Alba, precursor to medieval Scotland. From this background emerged the legend of the Gaelic warrior Ochonochar. Oral tradition relates that he grew up in Cé during the reign of Cenél Áed Find—Áed the White, or Áed mac Echdach—from 747 to 777 CE.

At that time, a great bear roamed the hillsides, or braes, of Cé. A well of pure water lay in a low-lying lagan between two high banks. Nine times, young Pict women attempted to draw water for their families, and nine times the bear mauled and killed them. This became known as the Nine Maidens' Well. Their families swore the surrounding land would be granted to anyone bold enough to rid the region of the monster.

Ochonochar accepted the challenge. Using his tracking and warrior skills, he found and slew the bear that had tormented the community. In doing so, he not only earned the land but also the epithet "Forbhasach," also spelled ferbash and ferbasach. This Gaelic term, meaning "bold man," literally means "large-headed" and idiomatically denotes someone "forward leaning"—one who stands boldly before others.

Ochonochar Forbhasach not only established a legend but also secured a homestead—dúthchas—for his kin group lasting more than a thousand years. The land became known in a shortened version as "Forbes," and his descendants were identified as "de Forbes," in the French Norman of the ruling class, or simply "of Forbes" in later English.

For generations, his saga survived in oral tradition through song and story until it was committed to manuscript in the great charter chest of his descendants. The tale recounts how Ochonochar slew the bear on the "Braes o' Forbes" near Logie. His lands still hold the first Castle Forbes— now called Druminnor Castle—in Rhynie, once the Pictish center of power for Cé.

Rise of the Clan

Society was organized around native kin-groups called clans—based on the Gelic word "clanna" or children. The early medieval northeast region known as Cé was governed by a Mormaer, or provincial authority just below a king, of the Clan Mar. As the ancient Gaelic power of Clan Mar waned in the 12th and 13th centuries, its former territories and responsibilities did not disappear; instead, they were assumed by rising local families who had long served as allied kindreds or septs within the wider Mar hegemony.

Among these, the early Forbeses emerged as the most prominent. The Forbes kindred gradually consolidated land, leadership, and military influence across the upper Don valley. By the late medieval period, they had transformed from a subordinate sept into a fully recognized independent clan, exercising the authority, territorial stewardship, and kinship leadership once held by the Mormaers themselves. In this way, Clan Forbes inherited not only land, but a mantle of regional guardianship—carrying forward the Gaelic traditions of Cé while establishing a distinct identity that would shape Aberdeenshire for centuries.

Clan Chiefs

The native Gaelic line of the Mormaers of Mar ended with the death of Thomas, 9th Earl of Mar, who died without heirs in 1377. Into that void stepped the formidable John, fifth laird of the land called Forbes after the legendary warrior Ochonochar Forbasach. Known as John of the "Black Lip" for a distinctive birthmark, this first clan chief of Forbes balanced loyalty to kin with the demands of royal justice as the king's representative in the region.

John married Elizabeth, daughter of Sir John Kennedy of Dunure, in 1375, forging ties with one of Scotland's most prominent Lowland families. John's union produced three sons who founded powerful branches of the House of Forbes: Alexander, the future 1st Lord Forbes; William, founder of the Pitsligo line; and John, progenitor of the

Tolquhon line. A fourth youth in the household, Alastair of Brux, was probably a "natural," or illegitimate, son. From him sprang the Skellater and Inverernan branches.

The line of clan chiefs continued for six and a half centuries to the current chief, Malcolm Nigel Forbes, 23rd Lord Forbes. He succeeded his father, Nigel Ivan Forbes, the 22nd Lord Forbes, in 2013, becoming the senior peer of the Forbes lineage and the current holder of the oldest Lordship of Parliament in Scotland.

Born into a family long associated with public service, military leadership, and stewardship of the Aberdeenshire homeland, Lord Forbes continues this tradition as custodian of Castle Forbes, the ancestral seat near the village of Alford.

His role as clan chief places him at the center of global Forbes heritage, where he is known for his steady, dignified leadership and his encouragement of all who seek connection with their Scottish roots. His grandson Geordie Malcolm Andrew Forbes is his heir apparent to the chiefship and is styled the Master of Forbes. (Both are pictured above.)

Today, Malcolm, 23rd Lord Forbes, remains an active symbol of the clan's enduring legacy—balancing tradition with modern engagement, and offering a unifying presence for Forbes descendants around the world.

Cadet Branches

Clan Forbes developed one of the most extensive family with cadet branches of any northeastern Gaelic clan, reflecting centuries of territorial expansion, military service, and strategic marriages. From the medieval heartland around the upper Don valley, the chiefly line gave rise to numerous cadet houses that established their own estates, reputations, and legacies across Aberdeenshire and beyond.

Among the most prominent are the Forbes of Tolquhon, renowned for their architectural patronage and the construction of Tolquhon Castle; the Forbes of Pitsligo, whose lords became noted statesmen and later Jacobite supporters; the Forbes of Craigievar, builders of the iconic Craigievar Castle and influential figures in royal administration; the Forbes of Corse, producing some of Scotland's most respected clerics as well as a noble family in Ireland; and the Forbes of Monymusk, long associated with scholarship, estate management, and cultural life in the Garioch. Other significant branches include the houses of Corsindae, Newe, Boyndlie, Foveran, and Skellater, each contributing distinct threads to the clan's political, military, and social history.

Together, these branches form the wider "House of Forbes," a network of kin-groups whose influence shaped the northeast for more than six centuries.

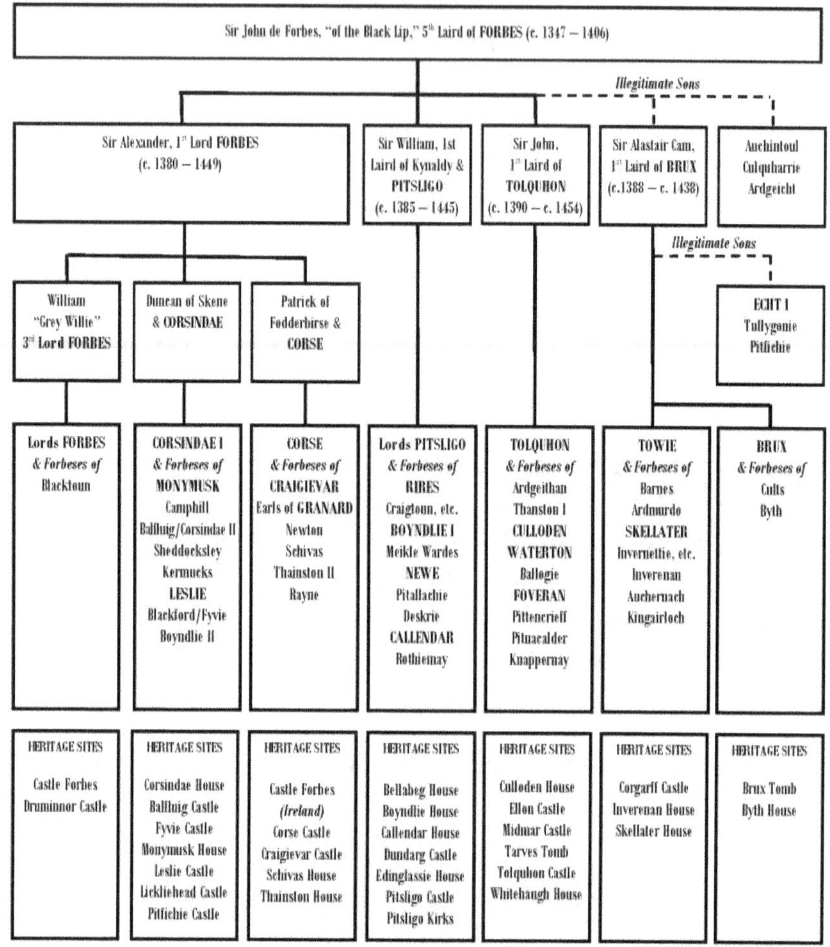
Sir John de Forbes, "of the Black Lip," 5th Laird of FORBES (c. 1347 – 1406)
Illegitimate Sons
Sir Alexander, 1st Lord FORBES (c. 1380 – 1449)
Sir William, 1st Laird of Kynaldy & PITSLIGO (c. 1385 – 1445)
Sir John, 1st Laird of TOLQUHON (c. 1390 – c. 1454)
Sir Alastair Cam, 1st Laird of BRUX (c.1388 – c. 1438)
Auchintoul
Culquharrie
Ardgeicht
Illegitimate Sons
William "Grey Willie" 3rd Lord FORBES
Duncan of Skene & CORSINDAE
Patrick of Fodderbirse & CORSE
ECHT I
Tullygonie
Pitfichie
Lords FORBES & Forbeses of Blacktoun
CORSINDAE I & Forbeses of MONYMUSK
Camphill
Balfluig/Corsindae II
Sheddocksley
Kermucks
LESLIE
Blackford/Fyvie
Boyndlie II
CORSE & Forbeses of CRAIGIEVAR
Earls of GRANARD
Newton
Schivas
Thainston II
Rayne
Lords PITSLIGO & Forbeses of RIRES
Craigtoun, etc.
BOYNDLIE I
Meikle Wardes
NEWE
Pitallachie
Deskrie
CALLENDAR
Rothiemay
TOLQUHON & Forbeses of Ardgeithan
Thanston I
CULLODEN
WATERTON
Ballogie
FOVERAN
Pittencrieff
Pitnacalder
Knappernay
TOWIE & Forbeses of Barnes
Ardmurdo
SKELLATER
Invernettie, etc.
Inverenan
Auchernach
Kingairloch
BRUX & Forbeses of Cults
Byth
HERITAGE SITES
Castle Forbes
Druminnor Castle
HERITAGE SITES
Corsindae House
Balfluig Castle
Fyvie Castle
Monymusk House
Leslie Castle
Lickliehead Castle
Pitfichie Castle
HERITAGE SITES
Castle Forbes (Ireland)
Corse Castle
Craigievar Castle
Schivas House
Thainston House
HERITAGE SITES
Bellabeg House
Boyndlie House
Callendar House
Dundarg Castle
Edinglassie House
Pitsligo Castle
Pitsligo Kirks
HERITAGE SITES
Culloden House
Ellon Castle
Midmar Castle
Tarves Tomb
Tolquhon Castle
Whitehaugh House
HERITAGE SITES
Corgarff Castle
Inverenan House
Skellater House
HERITAGE SITES
Brux Tomb
Byth House

The Land of Forbes

From the heartland of the upper Don valley, the clan's cadet branches spread across the Garioch, Strathdon, and the foothills of the Cairngorms, founding estates such as Tolquhon, Corse, Craigievar, Monymusk, Corsindae, Newe, Skellater, and Foveran. As the clan grew in prominence, its reach extended far beyond its ancestral homeland.

One of the most significant northern expansions was the establishment of the Forbeses of Culloden, near Inverness. Acquired in 1626 by "Grey Duncan" Forbes, this estate became a center of legal, political, and military leadership. To the south, the House of Forbes extended its influence into the Lowlands with the acquisition of Callendar Estate near Falkirk. From this base, the family expanded into Ayrshire, Dumfriesshire, and Galloway, establishing a southern sphere of Forbes landownership that endured well into the 20th century.

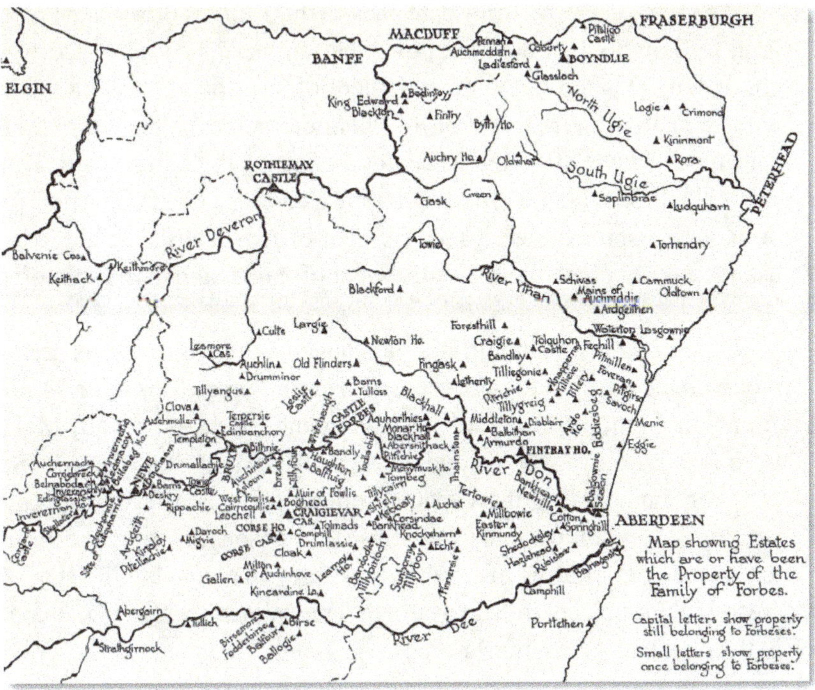

Symbols and Heraldry

Identity in the Gaelic world rested on kinship, territory, and personal allegiance, not on visual symbols. A chief was known by lineage and reputation, and a clan's authority was expressed through its people and its land rather than through heraldic devices.

As Scotland absorbed Norman feudal culture from the 12th century onward, the Forbeses—like many ancient Gaelic families—adapted to the new social order. With this transition came the adoption of heraldic symbols, including coats of arms, a clan motto, and eventually the crest badge used by modern clan members. These emblems did not replace the clan's Gaelic identity but rather became the outward signs of its status within the evolving political and cultural landscape of medieval Scotland.

The use of Coats of Arms date back to the 12th century when they were used by knights for identification. The number and variety led to great confusion. This led to the development of an official class of "heralds," who regulated the registration of "heraldic achievements" or "armorial bearings." James III established the office of the Lord Lyon, King of Arms, in 1437 who recorded and approved these Coats of Arms. While only one person may use a specific Coat of Arms, any clan member may use the family crest, the top of the Coat of Arms, above the shield.

Since French was the official language of the Norman monarchy, the motto on the Forbes of Forbes coat of arms is "Grace Me Guide," meaning "may grace guide me" or "let grace guide me." As explained by Malcolm, Lord Forbes, the motto "embodies a sense of duty" in all relations. Scores of other members of the cadet families of the House of Forbes have petitioned for their own coats of arms. While clan members are forbidden to use the coat of arms of Lord Forbes, they may display the stag on the crest of the arms encircled by a belt. This symbolizes their membership in the clan headed by Lord Forbes.

Forbes Coats of Arms

Forbes of Forbes

Forbes of Pitsligo

Forbes of Craigiever

Forbes of Newe

**Forbes of Monymusk,
1st to 5th Baronets**

**Forbes of Granard,
Earls of Ireland**

While the notion of "clan tartans" has been a relatively recent notion, our Celtic ancestors have been weaving a distinctive tartan cloth for millennia. In ancient Scotia, weavers used local plants for their dyes. The actual patterns were based on the availability and quantity of the dyed wool. Large swaths of tartan were used as "great kilts" (or "feileadh mòr" in Gaelic) and functioned as clothing, blanket, backpack, and tent. When called up for battle, Scotsmen would wear whatever tartan was woven into their great kilts.

However, when organizing these soldiers into regiments, some commanders required more uniformity. For example, The Tartan Authority notes that "The Laird of Grant (1704) gave instruction for his men-at-arms to wear a uniform tartan, as reported by a British Army officer." Since many regiments were comprised predominately of a single clan, this may be the origin of the concept of a "clan tartan."

While several retail businesses and weavers promote many different "Forbes" tartans, not all are actually recorded with the Scottish Register of Tartans. While anyone can wear whatever tartan they want, Clan Chief Malcolm, Lord Forbes, has determined that the only official Clan Forbes Tartan is designated as Scottish Tartan Authority (STA) number 211.

Other "symbols" of Clan Forbes were first published in the early twentieth century on the wave of romantic Scottish enthusiasm—only some of which are based on actual history.

The war cry of "Lonach!" is based on the notion that this cry would gather the clan to Lonach Hill, then one of the highest points in the region once called Forbes. Bounded on three sides by the River Don, the hill is marked by a cairn and a granite boundary stone with the letters "S" and "I" cut into the West-South-West and East-North-East sides respectively. This indicates the boundaries of the former Forbes estates of Skellater and Invernan.

This has been modified to "Ho Ho Lonach!" by the Lonach Highlanders (pictured below), a ceremonial body of men drawn from the Strathdon area of Aberdeenshire and organized under the Lonach Highland and Friendly Society, founded in 1823 by Sir Charles Forbes of Newe. They are best known for their annual ceremonial march from Bellabeg to Strathdon during the Lonach Highland Gathering and Games, held on the fourth Saturday of August.

The "official" bagpipe music noted in vintage books of Scottish heritage is "The Battle of Glen Eurann." However, no record exists of such a place or battle—and the music itself has never been found. Instead, the Lonach Pipe Band (Lonach Gu Bràth in Gaelic) has chosen "The Lonach March" as their anthem.

These antique tomes also list the Scotch broom as the Clan Forbes "badge." The popular belief is that clan members wore this plant badge in their bonnets to identify themselves in battle. While this notion is more folklore than fact, the Scotch broom has many qualities that may well suit the nature of the clan.

The Scotch broom is known for its resilience, adaptability, and vibrant presence. The plant thrives in harsh conditions, growing in poor soil and enduring tough climates. The plant spreads rapidly, with seed pods that burst open and disperse widely. Historically, Scotch broom provided cover for game and materials for thatching cottages.

Likewise, Clam Forbes has shown endurance through centuries of political and social upheaval, expanded its reach by establishing branches across Scotland and beyond, and long been associated with leadership and protection.

Whether historical fact or romantic fiction, the Clan Forbes badge of the Scotch broom is certainly an admirable choice.

Part II – Brief History

Wars of Scottish Independence

While the origin of the name Forbes may be shrouded in mystery and legend, the clan's legacy is boldly inscribed in the pages of Scottish history. Emerging from oral tradition, the Forbes family established its ancestral claim in law.

King Alexander III granted the dùthchas of "ye landis of Forbes and Kern" to Duncan de Forbeys in 1271/72. This recognition placed the Forbeses among the native landholding families who owed allegiance to the Mormaers of Mar, the Gaelic provincial rulers whose authority predated the feudal earldom.

Duncan de Forbes lived in relative stability under King Alexander III, but his heirs were thrust into the crucible of Scotland's Wars of Independence. Daring to face English steel rather than English rule, the Forbes line stood on the brink of extinction in service to Scottish independence. Twice, the family survived only through the posthumous births of the sons of freedom fighters, a legacy of sacrifice and resilience.

Sir John de Forbes, the 2nd laird, played a decisive role in the northern campaigns of Andrew de Moray and William Wallace, holding Urquhart Castle after its capture in 1297. Though the castle fell to English forces in 1303 after a "stout defence," Sir John escaped and later defended Kildrummy Castle for Robert the Bruce, dying in that service .

The next generation continued this legacy. John, 3rd laird of Forbes, fought for the rightful heir, David II, and fell at Dupplin Moor in 1332—another moment when the line survived only through a posthumous son. His child, John, 4th laird, so impressed King David II with his "sprightly and handsome personage" that the king knighted him as a youth and later confirmed Forbes lands across Aberdeenshire, including Edinbanchory, Craiglogie, Meikle Fintery, and Findrassie.

Battle of Harlaw and the Rise of Forbes

The eldest son of John, 4th laird of Forbes, was Sir John "of the Black Lip," who became the 5th laird of Forbes and first clan chief. At that time, Scotland was fractured between the Gaelic west and the feudal northeast. The Earldom of Ross, from Skye to Inverness-shire, became the center of a fierce succession dispute. When Euphemia II, Countess of Ross, inherited the title in 1402 under the protection of Robert Stewart, Duke of Albany, her claim was challenged by Donald of Islay, Lord of the Isles, whose marriage tied him to the earlier Ross line. Donald rallied the great western clans and swept eastward, capturing Dingwall and Inverness before marching toward Aberdeen.

Alexander Stewart, Earl of Mar, mustered the barons and clans loyal to the Crown—including the Leslies, Murrays, Straitons, and Forbeses. On July 24, 1411, the two forces clashed at the Battle of Harlaw, one of the bloodiest and most culturally symbolic battles in Scottish history.

Among Mar's warriors was Alexander Forbes (ca. 1380–1448), the eldest son of Sir John, "of the Black Lip." His valor at Harlaw was celebrated in later tradition, where the ballad *The Battle of Harlaw* praises "brave Forbes" for striking down MacDonald's champions. Poetic rather than literal, the song reflects the reputation Forbes earned on the field.

Alexander Forbes's loyalty and military service were richly rewarded. In 1423, the Earl of Mar granted him the lands of Alford, forming the nucleus of the modern-day Castle Forbes estate. His marriage in 1421 to Elizabeth Douglas, granddaughter of King Robert III, brought royal blood into the Forbes line. King James I later confirmed additional lands in Edinbanchory, Kearn, and Mar, and by 1442 Alexander Forbes was raised to the peerage as Lord Forbes, establishing the clan as one of the leading noble houses of Scotland.

Through courage at Harlaw, strategic alliances, and royal favor, the House of Forbes emerged from this turbulent era with land, title, and lineage—the foundations of its enduring prominence in Scottish history.

Rebellion Against King James III

Both Alexander's son, James, 2nd Lord Forbes, and grandson, William "Grey Willie," 3rd Lord Forbes, proved their loyalty to the crown on the field of the Battle of Brechin in 1452. Alexander Forbes succeeded his father, "Grey Willie," as the 4th Lord Forbes in 1483. Contemporary accounts described him as "one of the greatest Hectors of his age," reflecting his reputation as a formidable warrior and leader.

During the civil unrest of the late fifteenth century, Lord Forbes remained steadfastly loyal to King James III while much of the Scottish nobility rebelled. In recognition of this loyalty, the king entrusted Forbes with royal authority across northern Scotland, appointing him lieutenant over the districts beyond the Grampians and effectively placing regional governance in his hands.

Lord Forbes fought for the crown at the Battle of Sauchieburn in 1488, where James III was defeated and killed by forces supporting his own son, the future James IV. In the aftermath, Forbes rode through the north bearing the slain king's bloody shirt upon his spear, attempting to rally support for royal vengeance. Although he gathered a considerable force, resistance collapsed after further defeats among the king's supporters, bringing an end to organized opposition.

Despite his loyalty to the fallen monarch, Alexander Forbes received a pardon from James IV, who continued to rely upon the Lords Forbes in administering northern Scotland into the closing years of the century. This was a testament to the clan's enduring regional power and political importance. The career of the 4th Lord Forbes marked an important stage in the rise of the family as one of the dominant noble houses of northeastern Scotland. His royal appointments, military leadership, and continued authority under a new king helped secure the clan's standing for subsequent generations, laying a foundation that later Lords Forbes would build upon during the turbulent sixteenth century.

The Execution of the Master of Forbes

For most of the fifteenth century, Clan Forbes stood firmly allied with the Setons and Gordons, bound by shared military service and marriage. This partnership began when James, 2nd Lord Forbes, fought under the Alexander Seton (later Gordon,) 1st Earl of Huntly at the 1452 Battle of Brechin and so impressed him that Huntly offered his daughter, Christian Gordon, in marriage.

This alliance collapsed in 1525, when a violent feud with the Leslies drew the young John, Master of Forbes, into the killing of Alexander Seton of Meldrum, a kinsman of the Gordons. Outraged, Huntly had the Master of Forbes arrested, and only a massive fine secured his release. The breach between the families widened into open hostility.

In 1536, the Master of Forbes's cousin, John Strachan of Lenturk, enraged by a personal quarrel, informed the Earl of Huntly of fabricated charges that Forbes had plotted to kill King James V and aided the English. Both Lord Forbes and his son were imprisoned for treason.

Though the father was released, the Master of Forbes was tried in 1537, condemned on perjured testimony, and was beheaded in Edinburgh. As contemporary observers wrote, it was "one of the blackest forgeries that Hell could plot."

When he realized the perfidy, James V attempted to repair the damage. He restored the family's forfeited estates, brought the younger brother William Forbes into royal service as a gentleman of the bedchamber, and arranged his marriage to Elizabeth Keith in 1538. This royal favor marked the beginning of a cautious reconciliation between the Forbeses, the Crown, and their former allies.

Clan Forbes and Mary, Queen of Scots

The clan's relationship with Mary, Queen of Scots was one of the most complex and consequential chapters in its history. Although William, 7th Lord Forbes, was a committed Protestant, he initially supported the young Catholic queen. His kinsmen Arthur Forbes of Rires and Lady Margaret Beaton Forbes (Lady Reres)—a close companion of the Queen—remained loyal to Mary even to the point of committing murder.

Lord Forbes joined the Protestant lords in rejecting the proposed marriage between Mary and the son of King Henery VIII, signing the Secret Bond of 1543. In 1548, the Scottish Parliament agreed to the marriage treaty between Mary and three-year-old Francis, son and heir of King Henry II of France. For her safety, five-year-old Mary stayed at the French court. Mary and Francis were married in 1558 and became the rulers of France when Henry II died in 1559.

However, King Francis II died the next year in 1560, and Mary returned to Scotland in 1561. Her illegitimate half-brother, the James Stewart, 1st Earl of Moray, became her chief adviser. He ensured that members of Mary's new Privy Council included many Protestants. Enraged at the slight to his fellow Catholics, George Gordon, 4th Earl of Huntly, who served as the Lord Chancellor, led a rebellion against her.

Lord Forbes rallied to the Crown, fighting at Corrichie in 1562, where Huntly fell and his son was executed. For this loyalty, Mary granted Forbes a charter promising him Huntly's forfeited lands.

The Queen's later marriage to Lord Darnley, Darnley's murder, and her controversial union with the Earl of Bothwell pushed Scotland into open civil war. Forbes then supported the Earl of Moray, who became the Regent for her son, the young James VI.

Mary was first imprisoned in Scotland, escaped, and then fled to England where she was once again incarcerated by Queen Elizabeth. While he supported the young king, Forbes twice petitioned Queen Elizabeth for Mary's release.

In 1570, Moray was assassinated and three months later Moray's secretary was assassinated -- by Arthur Forbes, 4th of Rires and his two sons John and Arthur. The next Regent for the young King was Matthew Stewart, 4th Earl of Lennox. However, George Gordon, 5th Earl of Huntly, commanded a raid on Stirling Castle that resulted in the death of Lennox. This set the scene for a bloody feud between the Gordons and Forbeses for the next decade.

Forbes–Gordon Feud

The feud between the Gaelic Clan Forbes and the Norman House of Gordon became one of the most notorious conflicts in Scottish history. The feud reached its bloodiest phase in 1571, when Gordon forces ambushed the Forbeses at Tillieangus, killing thirty-six Forbes gentlemen and capturing many more. The violence continued with the burning of Corgarff Castle, where Margaret Campbell Forbes of Towie and her household perished, an atrocity immortalized in the ballad *Edom o' Gordon*.

Later that year, the clans clashed again at Craibstane, where the Master of Forbes was captured and imprisoned until the 1573 Pacification of Perth finally brought temporary peace.

Despite devastating losses, Clan Forbes emerged from the feud with its lands restored, its honor reaffirmed, and its political influence intact. The conflict became a defining chapter in Forbes identity—an enduring testament to the clan's resilience, loyalty to the Crown, and determination to defend its place in the north.

Covenanting Wars

The religious and political upheavals that followed the 1567 abdication of Mary, Queen of Scots eventually erupted into full-scale war in 1638. The conflict grew from deep tensions within the Kirk of Scotland, which had embraced Presbyterian reform under John Knox, while the Stuart kings—both James VI and his heir Charles I—attempted to impose episcopal control and English-style liturgy. In response, much of Scotland's nobility signed the National Covenant, pledging to defend the Kirk from royal interference. This effectively split power between the monarchy and the Covenanting nobility, who took control of the government. Clan Forbes aligned strongly with the Covenanter cause.

James Graham, 1st Marquess of Montrose, led the opposing Royalist forces. As Montrose advanced north, the Scottish government called out the Aberdeenshire levies. The local militia refused to follow Lord George Gordon, the eldest son and heir to George Gordon, 2nd Marquess of Huntly, and declared they would only follow Sir William Forbes of Craigievar. His force included numerous Forbes lairds—Tolquhon, Waterton, Monymusk, Echt, Corsindae, Leslie, and others—demonstrating the clan's unified commitment to the Covenant.

At the 1644 Battle of Aberdeen, Sir William led the Covenanter cavalry in a bold downhill charge, described as the work of the "fiery Forbeses," before being overwhelmed by Montrose's Irish musketeers. He survived, though several Forbeses were captured. Montrose continued his campaign through the northeast, briefly occupying Druminnor Castle, the ancestral seat of the Lords Forbes.

The following year, Forbes forces again faced Montrose at the 1645 Battle of Alford. The Covenanter army included cavalry commanded by Sir William Forbes of Craigievar, John Forbes of Leslie, and William, Master of Forbes (later 11th Lord Forbes). Despite their efforts, Montrose won a decisive victory. After Montrose's defeat at Philiphaugh, William, Master of Forbes, regained control of Druminnor, restoring the clan's authority in its ancestral heartland.

Jacobite Rebellion of 1689

Son of Charles I, King James II and VII was a committed Catholic and attempted to promote religious tolerance through measures such as the Declaration of Indulgence. However, many Protestant nobles viewed this as an attempt to undermine the established church and expand royal absolutism. These concerns intensified in 1688 with the birth of his son, also called James, raising the prospect of a lasting Catholic dynasty. In response, leading English and Scottish nobles invited the Protestant William of Orange—husband of James's daughter Mary—to intervene. William's successful invasion led to James's flight and the establishment of a new constitutional monarchy of William III and Mary II.

However, the new regime faced opposition from devoted Catholics and supporters of the deposed Stuart monarch. They were termed "Jacobites," from Jacobus, the Latin form of the name James. In 1689, this opposition turned into open rebellion when leaders such as John Graham of Claverhouse raised forces in the Highlands to restore James to the throne. The conflict quickly escalated into a military campaign.

Northeast Scotland was dominated by the Catholic Gordons who backed the exiled king. The exception was William, Master of Forbes and later 13th Lord Forbes, whom General Hugh Mackay, commander of the government forces, praised for his "unwearied perseverance" and "devoted attachment" to the Protestant cause. With his father, the elderly 12th Lord Forbes, William rallied Forbes allies and local levies, guarded key passes, and provided intelligence that helped drive Jacobite forces from the region.

The rebellion's single Jacobite victory came at Killiecrankie on July 27, 1689, where Viscount Dundee's Highland charge shattered Mackay's army—but Dundee was killed, leaving the Jacobite cause leaderless. The Master of Forbes continued to defend Aberdeenshire, and in 1690 he was promoted to lieutenant-colonel of a regiment of 600 Forbes clansmen, one of the few locally raised units loyal to monarchs William and Mary.

Jacobite Rebellion of 1715

When Queen Mary II died in 1694, her husband reigned as sole monarch until his own death in 1702. The crown went next to Mary's sister Anne. During her reign, the Parliament of England and the Parliament of Scotland passed the Acts of Union in 1707 to create Great Britain. When she died, the next Protestant in line was George of Hanover, the great-great-grandson of James VI & I. Jacobites were enraged that the crown did not go to James Francis Edward Stuart, the son of the deposed James VII and II.

John Erskine, Earl of Mar, (pictured here) was British Secretary of State under Queen Anne. However, George I dismissed him from office. Offended and ambitious, Mar raised the standard for "King James 3rd and 8th" at Braemar on September 6, 1715, igniting another Jacobite rebellion.

Officially, William, 13th Lord Forbes, supported the new Hanoverian regime and the Protestant succession. However, several prominent Forbeses chose the Jacobite side. James, the Master of Forbes (later 15th Lord Forbes) joined the Earl of Mar's rebellion, as did John Forbes of Boyndlie, who helped collect taxes in support of Mar's administration. Both Alexander Forbes, Lord Pitsligo, and John "Black Jock" Forbes of Inverernan emerged as determined Jacobite supporters.

The rebellion culminated in the Battle of Sheriffmuir on November 1715, an indecisive clash that nonetheless broke Jacobite momentum. James Stuart's late arrival in Scotland failed to revive the rebellion, and by early 1716 the movement collapsed. For Clan Forbes, the 1715 rebellion was not a simple story of loyalty or treason, but of a house divided. The episode left a lasting mark on the clan's memory, illustrating both its deep entanglement in national politics and the personal cost of choosing sides in a civil conflict.

Jacobite Rebellion of 1745

Thirty years after the failure of James Francis Edward Stuart to gain the throne, Jacobites found new hope in his son Charles Edward Stuart, popularly called "Bonnie Prince Charlie." Born in Italy to Scottish and Polish parents, Stuart was financially backed by the French and Spanish Catholic rulers who attempted to use Stuart to destabilize the government of Great Britain and install a client Catholic monarchy.

As in earlier rebellions, major branches of Clan Forbes stood on opposite sides. James, 15th Lord Forbes, who had once sympathized with the Jacobites in 1715, took no active role in 1745. His son, James, Master of Forbes (later 16th Lord Forbes), had already joined the British Army and served as a captain in the 25th Regiment of Foot.

Duncan Forbes, 5th Laird of Culloden, Lord President of the Court of Session, (pictured above) was a high-ranking leader in the British government. Through clan chiefs in the western isles, he first learned of the invasion and notified the government. He raised independent companies in the north, convinced many Highland clans to resist joining the rebellion, and coordinated government resistance from Inverness. Stuart seized his Forbes's home Culloden House and used the estate as his headquarters before the final battle.

The most prominent Jacobite Forbes was Alexander Forbes, 4th Lord Pitsligo, a respected statesman and veteran of the 1715 rising. At age 65, he returned to the Stuart cause and commanded the Jacobite cavalry as Master of Horse. Pitsligo fought at the 1746 Battle of Culloden, but escaped capture. His estates were forfeited, and his title attainted, but he remained a beloved figure among Jacobites until his death in 1762.

Duncan Forbes returned to find his home looted and his lands devastated. He never recovered financially and died the following year.

Part III — Heritage Sites

Druminnor Castle: First Castle Forbes

The first Forbes stronghold was Castle Forbes, later called Druminnor Castle. This was built on a fortification first established at some time before 1000 CE. In 1430, Alexander, 1st Lord Forbes, built a large hall block, the only part of the castle which has survived.

The castle has a tumultuous history: attacked by the Gordons in 1449; sacked by the Douglases in 1452; partially demolished by the Gordons again in 1571 through 1573; and frequently attacked by Jacobites in 1689, 1690, and 1746. To pay the growing family debts, James, 16th Lord Forbes, sold the castle in 1770.

Margaret Forbes-Sempill, a daughter of Lord Forbes-Sempill of Craigievar, bought Druminnor Castle in 1955. In 1975, Druminnor was bought by Andrew Forbes of the Pitsligo & Monymusk branch. The current owner is Andrew's son, Alexander Forbes.

Druminor Castle thumbnail sketches, National Records of Scotland

Castle Forbes

Castle Forbes is the seat of the clan and the private home of Malcolm and Jinny, Lord and Lady Forbes. The estate stands on land first granted to Sir Alexander Forbes in 1411 for his role in the Battle of Harlaw. After the sale of Druminnor in 1770, the Forbes family moved to Putachie House, which was rebuilt into the modern Castle Forbes.

Between 1807 and 1818, James Ochoncar, 17th Lord Forbes, transformed the house into a grand Scottish baronial residence. The project passed through several architects—John Paterson, Archibald Simpson, and finally John Smith—each leaving their mark as the old house was incorporated into the new. Portions of the earlier structure, likely dating to around 1600, can still be seen between the square and round towers. Between 1805 and 1814, Lord Forbes planted over 6.8 million trees on the estate.

In the early 20th century, Atholl, 21st Lord Forbes, modernized the castle with bathrooms, central heating, and electricity generated by a turbine on the River Don. During the Second World War, Castle Forbes served the nation as an Auxiliary Hospital for recovering servicemen. After the war, Lady Mabel Forbes remained in residence while her son, Nigel, 22nd Lord Forbes, managed the wider estate. In 1973, he gifted the castle and policies to his eldest son, Malcolm, then Master of Forbes.

Beginning in the 1990s, he restored the front entrance, rebuilt the courtyard, and converted the old dairy barn, briefly the site of the Castle Forbes perfumery. Today, Castle Forbes remains a working family home. Clan members are warmly welcomed, but visits must be arranged in advance out of respect for the family's privacy.

Pitsligo Castle

Sir William Forbes of Kynaldy, (c. 1385–1445), the younger brother of Alexander, 1st Lord Forbes, founded one of the most important cadet branches of the clan. In 1423 he married Agnes Fraser, heiress of Philorth, and soon after received a charter from James Douglas, Lord of Balveny, granting him lands in the barony of Aberdour once held by her family. By 1429, William's holdings were substantial enough to form a free barony, and he became known as Sir William Forbes, 1st Laird of Pitsligo.

Sir William began construction of Pitsligo Castle around 1424, starting with the tower and courtyard wall. Datestones reveal centuries of expansion and repair: 1577 likely marks restoration after Gordon attacks in the early 1570s, while stones dated 1603 and 1663 show continued additions to the entrance and garden walls. In 1634, Alexander Forbes, 9th Laird of Pitsligo, secured an Act of Parliament creating the parish of Pitsligo from his own estates and built Pitsligo Kirk with its family burial vault. The following year he was created 1st Lord Pitsligo.

The later Lords Pitsligo became devoted supporters of the Stuart cause. Alexander Forbes, 4th Lord Pitsligo, fought in both the 1715 and 1745 Jacobite risings. After the 1746 Battle of Culloden, the estate—already bankrupt—was forfeited, the castle ransacked, and Lord Pitsligo declared an outlaw. Protected by the loyalty of his tenants, he evaded capture and died peacefully in 1762.

Tolquhon Castle

Now a romantic ruin, Tolquhon Castle (pronounced toh-HON) was once one of the grandest residences in Aberdeenshire. Its story begins in 1420, when Sir John Forbes, third son of Sir John "of the Black Lip," married Mariota Preston, heiress of the Thane of Fermartyn. With their marriage came the lands of Tolquhon and the construction of Preston's Tower, the earliest part of the castle.

Tolquhon's most dramatic transformation came between 1584 and 1589, when William Forbes, 7th Lord of Tolquhon, rebuilt the castle as an elegant Renaissance courtyard house. Working with mason-architect Thomas Leper, he retained the medieval tower but added a grand gatehouse flanked by decorative gun-loop towers. A carved panel proudly records: "Al this warke… was begun be William Forbes 15 Aprile 1584 and endit… 20 October 1589."

Tolquhon remained in Forbes hands until the early 1700s. Sir Alexander Forbes, 10th Lord, a Royalist hero at the Battle of Worcester, later squandered the estate through scandal, lawsuits, and heavy investment in the disastrous Darien Scheme. Crushed by debt, the family lost the castle in 1716, and it passed through several owners before being abandoned in the 19th century. In 1929, Tolquhon Castle entered state care, preserving the evocative ruins that stand today.

Corse Castle

Now a ruin, Corse Castle once anchored a powerful Forbes estate in northeast Scotland. Its story begins with Patrick Forbes, younger son of the 2nd Lord Forbes and armor-bearer to King James III. In 1476, the king granted him the Barony of O'Neil and Corse, establishing

the Forbeses of Corse. Patrick's son David "Trail the Axe" succeeded him, followed by David's son Patrick, 3rd of Corse, and then William Forbes, 4th Lord of Corse, who married Elizabeth Strachan of Thornton.

Gordon raids in the 1570s damaged the old house at Corse, prompting Sir William to build a new fortified residence beginning in 1581. A stone above the doorway still bears his initials WF, the date, and those of his wife ES. Sir William famously declared he would build "such a house as thieves will need to knock at ere they enter."

Corse became the birthplace of several notable Forbeses. William's eldest son, Patrick Forbes (1564–1635), was born before the rebuilding and later served as Bishop of Aberdeen. Another son, William, purchased and completed Craigievar Castle, founding that distinguished line. A third son, John, also entered the church, while a sixth son, Arthur, established the Forbes baronets and earls in Ireland.

Patrick's son, theologian John Forbes (1593–1648), inherited Corse in 1635 but suffered exile for opposing the National Covenant. The castle was eventually abandoned in the mid-19th century when a modern mansion replaced it. The estate later passed through several generations, culminating in Sir James Forbes of Corse and Craigievar, 14th Baronet.

Craigievar Castle

The seven-story Craigievar Castle is one of the finest surviving examples of original Scottish Baronial architecture.

Its creator was William Forbes, son of the 4th Lord of Corse and brother of Patrick, Bishop of Aberdeen. Early in life William was a financial failure—despite generous loans from his brother—but he rebuilt his fortune through Baltic trade based in Danzig (now Gdańsk, Poland), earning him the nickname "Danzig Willy."

In 1610, Forbes purchased the unfinished Craigievar Castle from the bankrupt Mortimer family and completed it in 1626. The castle originally included a defensive courtyard with four round towers; only one survives today. William died the following year.

His son, also Sir William, used the family wealth to secure a Nova Scotia baronetcy in 1630, part of King James VI's scheme to fund colonization. The title passed to his only son, "Red" Sir John, 2nd Baronet, whose descendants continued the line. Through marriage, the Forbeses of Craigievar later connected with the Lords Sempill and the Lords Forbes. By the early 1800s, the tower had deteriorated. Sir John Forbes, 7th Baronet, considered demolishing it but was persuaded by architect John Smith to restore the structure, preserving what he called "one of the finest specimens" of its age.

In 1963, burdened by debt and death duties, William Forbes, 10th Baronet and 19th Lord Sempill, transferred Craigievar Castle and its policies to the National Trust for Scotland. The tower was reharled between 2008 and 2010, returning it to its historic rosy hue.

Corgarff Castle

Built around 1550 by John Forbes of Towie, Corgarff Castle began as a simple tower house within a rectangular enclosure. Its peaceful setting belies its place in one of the most tragic chapters of Forbes history, immortalized in the ballad "Edom o' Gordon."

During the civil conflict that followed the imprisonment of Mary, Queen of Scots, the Forbeses supported the young James VI, while the Gordons backed Mary's claim. In 1571, Adam Gordon of Auchindoun—the "Edom" of the ballad—defeated Forbes forces at Tillieangus and Craibstone, leaving the region vulnerable. With the Forbes army scattered, Gordon sent Captain Thomas Kerr to seize Corgarff. Lady Margaret Campbell Forbes, wife of John Forbes of Towie, refused to surrender. Gordon ordered the castle burned, killing Lady Towie, her children, and several attendants. The ballad mourns: *"Oh pity on yon fair castle,/ That was biggit wi' stane and lime… / And wae for Lady Campbell herself, / Burnt wi' her bairnies nine."*

Corgarff reappeared in history during the Jacobite Rising of 1715, when the Earl of Mar used it as a staging point. After his defeat, government troops burned the castle again and later seized the estate.

In 1746, George Forbes of Skellater sold Corgarff to the British Government, which transformed it into a military outpost. The distinctive star-shaped wall, pierced with gun loops, dates from this period. The garrison remained active until 1831, after which the tower served as a distillery and later worker housing.

Corgarff stayed within the Delnadamph estate until 1961, when it passed into state care. Today, the castle is preserved by Historic Scotland and is open to visitors exploring its dramatic past.

Culloden House

Culloden House stands on the site of a 16th-century fortified residence that witnessed some of the most turbulent moments in Scottish history. The estate appears in records as early as 1232 and was later claimed by Robert II, son of Robert the Bruce. Culloden passed through the Edmundson, Strachan, and Macintosh families before being purchased in 1626 by "Grey" Duncan Forbes, Provost of Inverness and nephew of the builder of Tolquhon Castle.

In 1688, Jacobite troops, seeking to restore the Stuart monarchy, plundered the estate. As compensation, the government granted Duncan Forbes, 3rd Laird of Culloden, a perpetual exemption allowing him to distill whisky at Ferintosh—creating Scotland's first legal distillery.

Culloden again came under attack in 1745, though the Forbes defenders repelled the Fraser raiders. At the time, the estate belonged to Duncan Forbes, 5th Laird Culloden, Lord President of the Court of Session. He raised troops against the Jacobites, but in 1746, the house was seized and pillaged by forces of Charles Edward Stuart, "Bonnie Prince Charlie," before their defeat at the Battle of Culloden.

Crushed by debt and never reimbursed for his wartime expenses, Duncan Forbes died in 1747. His son John Forbes, 6th Laird Culloden, revived the family fortunes through whisky production and rebuilt Culloden House between 1772 and 1788. The Forbes family held the estate until 1897. In 1975, Culloden House was transformed into the elegant country-house hotel that welcomes visitors today.

Bunchrew House

Bunchrew House—from the Gaelic Bun Chraoibh, "foot of the tree"—was the birthplace and favored residence of Duncan Forbes, 5th Laird of Culloden, the influential Lord President of the Court of Session.

The estate's story begins around 1615, when Simon Fraser, 6th Lord Lovat, built a fortified house on the site, complete with moat and drawbridge. After his death in 1633, the property remained with the Frasers until John Forbes, 2nd Laird of Culloden, purchased it around 1669 from Simon Fraser of Inverallochy.

Portions of the original 17th-century structure still stand at the western end of the house, though the moat and drawbridge have long vanished. In the 19th century, substantial additions expanded the building to the north and south.

The Forbes family left a lasting mark on the estate. John Forbes traveled widely and planted exotic trees across the grounds, including magnificent cedars that still dominate the landscape. His son Duncan Forbes, 3rd Laird of Culloden, fathered two sons: "Bumper John," who died without issue, and Duncan Forbes, the future Lord President, who made Bunchrew his home for more than three decades. Today, Bunchrew House is a four-star hotel set amid 20 acres of gardens.

Callendar House

Set within the sweeping grounds of Callendar Park in Falkirk, Callendar House stands directly on the line of the Antonine Wall, the 2nd-century Roman frontier from the Firth of Clyde to the Firth of Forth.

By the 12th century, the site was home to Thane House, seat of the Thanes of Callendar. Through marriage, the estate passed to the powerful Livingston family, who built the earliest surviving portion of the present house—a 14th-century tower. The family's fortunes collapsed after the Jacobite Rebellion of 1715, when the 5th Earl of Linlithgow and 4th Earl of Callendar was attainted for treason and lost his titles and estates. His heir, William Boyd, 4th Earl of Kilmarnock, met the same fate after the 1745 Jacobite Rebellion.

In 1783, the forfeited Callendar estates were auctioned. The winning bidder was William "Copperbottom" Forbes (1756–1823), a cadet of the Newe Forbes line who amassed a vast fortune sheathing Royal Navy ships in copper. Forbes transformed Callendar House, expanding the mansion and creating formal gardens. Later generations continued to remodel the house, blending French Renaissance and Scottish Baronial styles.

Although the family sold the house and park to Falkirk in 1963, they retain much of the surrounding estate. Today, Callendar House remains a landmark of Forbes heritage and Scottish history.

Part IV – Beyond Scotland

Denmark

William Forbes of Helsingør became a successful Danish merchant in during the Sundtoldstiden, the "Sound Toll Era from" 1429 to 1857. This was when Danish King Eric of Pomerania imposed a toll on every foreign ship passing through the Øresund (the Sound).

William Forbes, known in Danish records as Willum Forbus, was one of the earliest Scots to establish himself there. He was in Aberdeenshire before 1474, likely the grandson of Duncan Forbes, an illegitimate son of Sir William Forbes, 1st Laird of Pitsligo. Like many Scots seeking opportunity abroad, he ventured to Denmark around 1500, first settling in Ålborg as a merchant associated with the Abbey of Our Lady.

Forbes later rose to prominence in Helsingør, where a sizeable Scottish community worshipped at St. Olaf's Church. He married Johanne Thomasdotter and their daughter Karine Forbes married Henrik Mogensen Rosenvinge, mayor of Elsinore and Bailiff of Bergenhus.

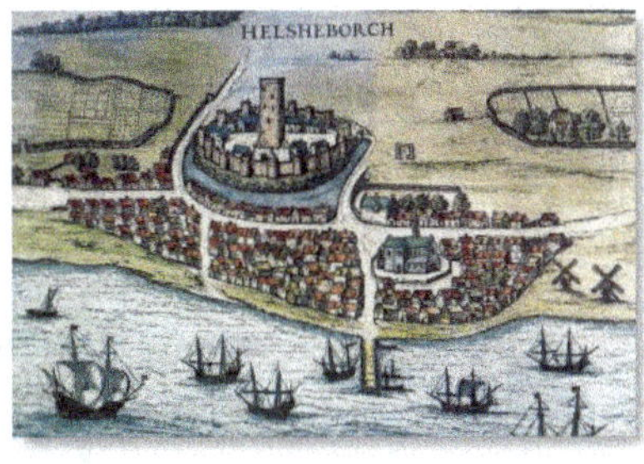

His father served Prince Christian—later King Christian II of Denmark, Norway, and briefly Sweden.

In 1529, King Frederick I granted Forbes land at Falsterbro in Skåne. After his wife's death in 1549, Forbes moved across the Øresund to Helsingør and later Helsingborg, where he lived until his death in 1561. That same year, Forbes's son-in-law confirmed to Duncan Forbes of Monymusk that "Blessed Willum Forbes in Helsingborg" descended from the Forbeses of Pitsligo. As a result, the Lord Lyon King of Arms authorized him to bear the Pitsligo symbols—three muzzled bear heads and the strawberry fraise—establishing the first recognized Forbes bloodline in Denmark.

Sweden and Finland

The presence of the Forbes family in Sweden and Finland highlights the military dimension of Scotland's global diaspora. The many branches of the family of Forbes were represented in the troops of Swedish King Gustavus Adolphus by no less than some 40 members.

The first Forbes in Swedish military service appears to have been Henry Forbes of Tolquon, who fell at Kirkholm in Russia in 1605. His eldest son, Jakob Forbes, was the first of the Swedish family Forbes of Lund. The younger son, Peter Forbes, became a paymaster of the army.

In the 17th century, Ernald Forbes of Corsindae migrated to Finland (part of Sweden until 1917), via Mecklenburg. He had two sons, Arvid and Mattias. They entered Swedish service and were naturalized into the Swedish nobility in 1638. Mattias served primarily in regional administration and estate management in Österbotten, supporting Sweden's expanding military state. He acted as a local magistrate and landholder, strengthening the family's influence in Finland during a period of intense political and military change.

Arvid (pictured here) began his career as a lieutenant in Ernst Creutz's Nyland Regiment (1623–1626) before rising to captain and lieutenant colonel in the Björneborg Regiment by 1630. He distinguished himself in the Thirty Years' War, serving as colonel and fighting at Nördlingen (1634). From 1635 he served under Duke Bernhard of Saxe-Weimar and helped secure the surprise victory at Rheinfelden in 1638.

His success led to major appointments, including commandant of Stralsund, major general, and vice-governor of Pomerania. He later built a notable residence in Stockholm. Forbus died in 1665, remembered as a leading Finnish-born officer of Sweden's imperial era.

Ireland: The Earls of Granard

Arthur was born in 1569 to William Forbes, 4th Laird of Corse, as the sixth son. His elder brothers included Patrick, later Bishop of Aberdeen; Sir William Forbes of Menie and Craigevar; and Rev. John Forbes of Corse. He served in the Master of Forbes' regiment in Ireland. For his service, Sir Arthur was granted in 1620 by "the commission of King James I., for planting the country," 1,268 acres in Counties Leitrim and Longford, including a barony called Castle Forbes. Along with his other brothers James and Robert, he was naturalized as a "free denizen" of Ireland in 1622. That same year, he married Jane Lauder of the Bass. Their eldest son, Arthur, was born about 1623.

Created a Baronet of Nova Scotia in 1628, Forbes later served in Germany under Gustavus Adolphus during the Thirty Years' War. He was killed in a duel at Hamburg in 1632.

During Arthur's absences abroad, his wife Jane oversaw the construction of Castle Forbes. She defended the castle for nine months during a siege in 1641 by Irish rebel forces, but she ultimately surrendered to the Confederate army under General Thomas Preston.

Although only 18, the younger Arthur had raised men and attempted to come to his mother's relief during the siege, but after the surrender went to Scotland and joined the Royalist party under James Graham, Marquess of Montrose. He was taken prisoner and suffered a long imprisonment in Edinburgh. He was released after the battle of Kilsyth. This engagement of the Wars of the Three Kingdoms was fought in 1645 and resulted in a decisive Royalist victory by Montrose, against the Covenanter army commanded by General William Baillie.

After the Restoration of Charles II in 1660, Sir Arthur was given a commission in the King's Forces and, in 1670, appointed Privy Councillor of Ireland and Commander-in-Chief of the Army in Ireland. On September 23rd, 1675, he was created Baron Clanehugh and Viscount Granard in the Kingdom of Ireland. In 1684, King Charles II bestowed the title of Earl of Granard. He died in 1696.

Subsequent earls continued this service. Arthur, 2nd Earl of Granard (1656–1734), held senior commands in Ireland and served in the Irish House of Lords. George, 3rd Earl of Granard, (1685–1765), was a respected Irish peer and military officer. He modernized the family estates and served actively in the Irish Parliament. George, 4th Earl of Granard, (1710–1769), held positions in the Irish House of Lords and maintained the Granard estates during a period of agricultural and economic change.

George, 5th Earl of Granard, (1740–1780), served as an Irish peer during the politically turbulent pre-Union era. His early death left the title to his son, George, 6th Earl of Granard (1760–1837). He guided the family through the Act of Union and early nineteenth-century reforms. George, 7th Earl of Granard, (1794–1836), served as an Anglo-Irish nobleman during the post-Union era and his early death left the title to his young son, George Hastings Forbes, 8th Earl of Granard (1833–1889). He became a prominent Victorian peer known for his interest in estate development and Irish affairs.

Bernard Arthur William Patrick Hastings Forbes, 9th Earl of Granard, (1874–1948), was a distinguished diplomat and military officer. He served as a British representative in Paris, married American heiress Beatrice Mills, and revitalized the family's fortunes. Arthur Patrick Hastings Forbes, 10th Earl of Granard, (1915–1992), served in the Irish Guards during World War II and later managed the family's Irish and American interests. Peter Arthur Edward Hastings Forbes, 11th Earl of Granard, (born 1957) continues the Granard legacy into the twenty-first century.

Australia

The story of the House of Forbes in Australia reflects the broader currents of Scottish migration across the British Empire. Scots were among the earliest Europeans connected to the continent: Lieutenant James Cook, son of a Scottish ploughman, charted Australia's east coast in 1770, paving the way for British settlement. After the American Revolutionary War ended convict transportation to North America, Britain established a new penal colony at Botany Bay. The First Fleet arrived in January 1788, carrying the first Forbes in Australia—prisoner Ann Forbes who had been sentenced to seven years.

Scottish influence grew quickly. Captain John Hunter became Governor of New South Wales in 1795, and Major General Lachlan Macquarie—later hailed as the "Father of Australia"—oversaw major reforms and public works between 1810 and 1822. By 1830, Scots made up roughly 15% of the colonial population, rising through waves of assisted emigration and the Highland Potato Famine.

The most distinguished Forbes in Australia was Sir Francis William Forbes (1784–1841), the colony's first Chief Justice. A reformer and legal architect, he helped draft the New South Wales Act of 1823, ensured colonial laws aligned with English law, and championed public education, laying the foundation stone of Sydney College. His legacy endures in the town of Forbes and the Francis Forbes Society for Australian Legal History.

Australia quickly became a destination for free settlers seeking economic opportunity. Among these were thousands of Scots, including members of the extended Forbes family. By 2016, over 2 million Australians—approximately 8.6% of the population—claimed Scottish ancestry, underscoring the enduring cultural imprint of this migration.

Forbes descendants contributed to the development of colonial and modern Australia, participating in commerce, agriculture, and civic life.

James Forbes of Hartford, Connecticut

James Forbes (1627–1692) stands among the earliest members of the House of Forbes to settle in North America. Likely the son of Captain James Forbes of Caithness and grandson of Duncan Forbes of Culloden, he was swept into the turmoil of the Wars of the Three Kingdoms. In 1650 he fought for Charles II at the Battle of Dunbar, where the Scots were defeated and more than 10,000 prisoners captured. Many, including Forbes, were shipped to New England as indentured servants. One of the names on the passenger list was "James farfason," almost certainly a clerk's rendering of Forbes.

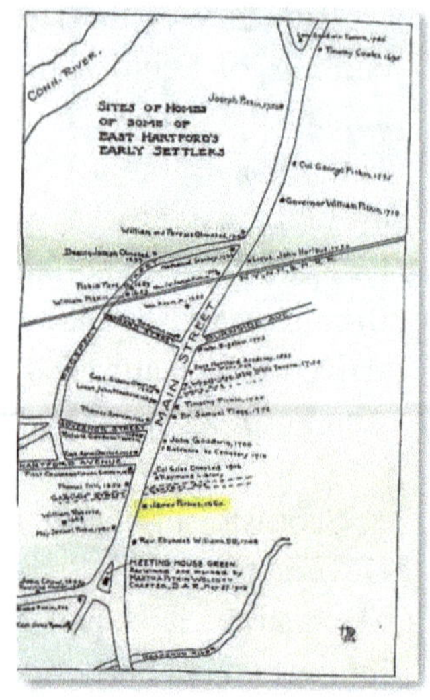

By 1658, Forbes was recorded in Hartford, working on a local farm and soon acquiring land of his own. His early deeds spell his name "fforbas" and describe "One parcell of Meadow lying on the East side of the great River." Over the next three decades he steadily expanded his holdings, ultimately owning a house, barn, pasture, woodland, meadow, and swampland valued at £344.

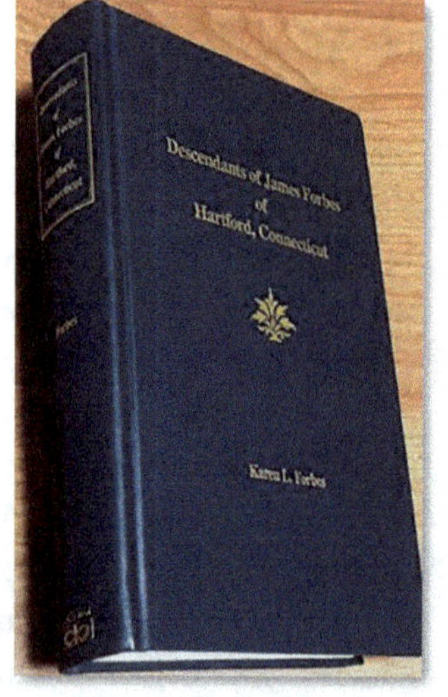

By 1688, Forbes and his family lived in the Hartford neighborhood known as "Scotland." At his death in 1692, he left seven children whose numerous descendants spread across North America. Their lineage is meticulously traced in Karen Lorraine Forbes's genealogy, *Descendants of James Forbes of Hartford, Connecticut.*

William Forbes/Furbish: Prisoner of War, Maine

William Forbes—later recorded as Furbish, Furbush, or Ferbish—was born in Aberdeen on 8 May 1631. He was swept into the Wars of the Three Kingdoms. On September 3, 1650, William and his brother Daniel fought for Scotland at the Battle of Dunbar, where English Oliver Cromwell's "New Model Army" crushed the Scottish army. Thousands were marched south as prisoners; many died along the way or later in the horrific conditions at Durham Cathedral. Of the 3,500 men imprisoned there, 1,700 perished due to the harsh conditions.

To dispose of surviving prisoners, the English Council of State shipped 150 of the strongest to New England aboard the *Unity* in late 1650. Sold as an indentured servant, William likely served his term in Dover, New Hampshire, where he first appears in records in 1659. After gaining his freedom, he acquired 80 acres along the Piscataqua River in what became Eliot, Maine—land that would anchor the Furbish family for generations.

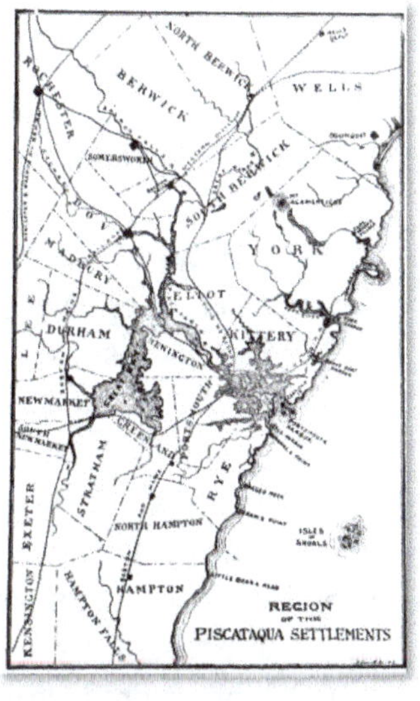

A fiercely independent Scotsman, William repeatedly clashed with Puritan authorities. He was fined for defending persecuted Quaker women, for resisting a constable, and once received twenty lashes for calling officials "Divells and hell Hounds." Yet he also became a substantial landowner, husband to Rebecca, and father of seven children whose descendants spread throughout southern Maine. William made his will in 1694 and died soon after. His family appears among the Quaker households of Kittery by 1721. Today, thousands of Americans trace their lineage to this indomitable Forbes who survived war, captivity, and exile to build a new life in New England.

Forbes of Iron, Connecticut

For two generations, the Forbes family of Connecticut shaped the early American iron industry and supplied the new nation with essential materials for war and expansion. Samuel Forbes (1729–1827) (pictured here), grandson of James Forbes of Hartford and descendant of the Forbes of Culloden, began his career in the family forge on the Blackberry River after his father John purchased the works in 1751.

By 1759, the Seymour Iron Works was fully in Forbes hands, with Samuel and his brother Elisha expanding production across East Canaan. In 1746, John established a blacksmith shop for his then 17-year-old son Samuel, marking the beginning of Samuel's long leadership in the trade.

After Elisha's death in 1765, Samuel became sole proprietor and built a vertically integrated iron empire—controlling ore beds, charcoal supplies, skilled labor, and standardized production. This system proved vital during the Revolutionary War, when the Connecticut government urged him to produce cannon, shot, kettles, and weapons parts. The furnace produced an extraordinary amount of heavy and light cannon during the Revolutionary War.

Following the war, Samuel partnered with his son-in-law John Adam to form Forbes & Adam, supplying nail rod, refined iron, anchors for the U.S. Navy, and parts for Eli Whitney's groundbreaking firearms. By his death in 1827, Samuel Forbes had become a regional industrial titan whose enterprises powered America's early growth.

Forbes Purchase, West Florida

John Forbes of Gamrie Parish, Banffshire, born to James Forbes and Sarah Gordon, emerged as one of the most influential Forbes figures in early American frontier commerce. John's elder brother Thomas joined their uncle John Gordon in Charleston, where Gordon's trading firm eventually evolved into the powerful Panton, Leslie & Company—founded by Scots William Panton, Thomas Forbes, John Leslie, William Alexander, and Charles McLatchy. By the 1780s, the company dominated Native American trade from St. Augustine to Pensacola.

When Florida returned to Spanish control in 1783, Panton, Leslie & Company convinced Spanish officials that their influence with the Creek, Choctaw, Chickasaw, Cherokee, and emerging Seminole peoples was essential to regional stability. John Forbes joined the firm in 1784, became a partner in 1792, and after William Panton's death in 1801 reorganized the enterprise as John Forbes & Company.

As Native Nations fell deep into debt, Forbes negotiated land cessions in exchange for settling their obligations. Between 1805 and 1814, these transactions produced the vast Forbes Purchase, more than 1.4 million acres stretching from Apalachicola Bay into present-day Liberty, Franklin, Leon, Wakulla, and Gadsden Counties. It became the largest land grant in Spanish

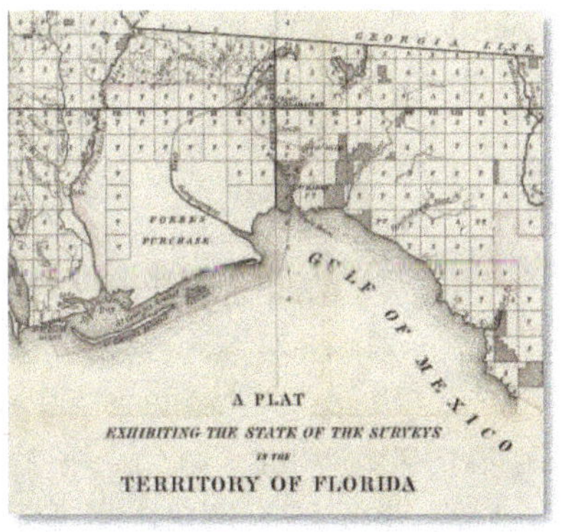

Florida. Though later mired in legal battles, the Forbes Purchase remains memorialized today in Forbes Island and Forbes Street in Apalachicola. John Forbes retired to Cuba, where he died in 1823, leaving a legacy of extraordinary commercial and political influence in the southeastern borderlands.

Brahmin Forbes Family of Boston

The Boston Forbes family descended from the Forbes of Newe through the Rev. John Forbes (1740–1783), son of John Forbes of Deskrie and Margaret Farquharson. Educated at King's College, Aberdeen, he became minister at St. Augustine, East Florida, in 1763. During a visit to Boston in 1769, he married Dorothy Murray, daughter of prominent merchant James Murray, linking the Forbes line to the rising "Boston Brahmin" elite. Loyal to the Crown during the American Revolution, Rev. Forbes returned to England in 1783, while Dorothy raised their three sons— James Grant, John Murray, and Ralph Bennet—in Boston.

Ralph Bennet Forbes married Margaret Perkins, connecting the family to the immense mercantile empire of Thomas Handasyd Perkins, whose fortune spanned the slave trade, the China Trade, and the opium traffic. Their sons—Thomas Tunno, Capt. Robert Bennet (Ben) Forbes,  and John Murray Forbes—became central figures in America's commercial expansion. Captain Ben Forbes entered the China Trade at age thirteen, later commanding the opium depot ship *Lintin* and serving as U.S. vice-consul at Canton. His brother John Murray Forbes shifted from the China Trade to railroads, becoming a leading figure in the Michigan Central and the Chicago, Burlington & Quincy lines.

In 1847, the brothers led America's first international humanitarian mission, sailing the *USS Jamestown* to deliver famine relief to Ireland. John later became a key Republican political figure and supporter of Abraham Lincoln. The family seat in Milton, Massachusetts—built in 1833 and transformed into the Forbes House Museum in 1964—preserves their legacy through China Trade collections and Mary Bowditch Forbes's extensive Lincoln memorabilia.

Forbes in Colonial New Jersey

John Forbes of Aquorthies—descended from the Forbes of Balfluig and Boyndlie—became one of the earliest Scottish proprietors and settlers in East Jersey during the Quaker-led colonization of the 1680s. A devoted Quaker, Forbes had already been fined and imprisoned a number of times in Aberdeen for attending illegal conventicles, and his religious convictions aligned him with Robert Barclay of Urie, the leading Quaker theologian and titular Governor of East Jersey. The Forbes and Barclay families were closely intertwined through several marriages.

In 1683, Barclay and fellow Quaker proprietors—including powerful Scottish statesmen such as the Earl of Perth and Lord Tarbat—commissioned the ship *Exchange* to carry settlers to East Jersey. Among the emissaries sent to survey the colony were David Barclay and Arthur Forbes, John's brother. Their glowing report, published in *An Advertisement Concerning the Province of East-New-Jersey* (1684), encouraged Scots to emigrate.

Inspired by their account, John Forbes purchased a one-tenth proprietary share in July 1684 and embarked for America. After surviving a violent Atlantic storm and an unintended landing in Virginia, he traveled overland to East Jersey and settled near Cedar Brook at the Blue Hills. There he joined other prominent Scots—including the Gordons of Straloch and John Barclay, the governor's brother—and developed more than 1,600 acres acquired between 1684 and 1686.

Although Forbes never intended permanent settlement, he improved his lands, appointed an agent, and returned to Scotland in 1686. His brief but influential presence helped establish a strong Scottish and Quaker foundation in early New Jersey, marking him as one of the first Forbes pioneers in colonial America.

Forbes Silversmiths of New York

The New York branch of the Forbes family built one of early America's most enduring silversmithing dynasties. Their story begins with William Forbes, a Scottish immigrant who settled in New York around 1703. Though a cordwainer by trade, his descendants—through his son Gilbert Forbes—established a multigenerational lineage of master silversmiths whose work now resides in major museums and private collections.

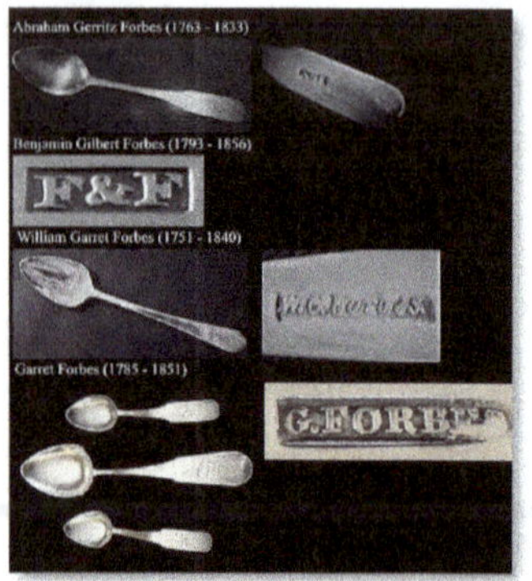

Gilbert's sons William Garret Forbes (1751–1840) and Abraham Gerritze Forbes (1763–1833) founded the family's silversmithing tradition around 1785. William Garret, a freeman of New York City and member of the Gold and Silversmith's Society, produced elegant trays, tea services, and flatware influenced by his Scottish and Dutch heritage. A proven Patriot, he served in the powder house guard in 1775. His hallmark, "W. G. Forbes," remains highly collectible.

The craft passed to the next generation: Garret Forbes, John Wolfe Forbes, and Colin Van Gelder Forbes—all sons of William Garret—became prominent silversmiths. John Wolfe's ornate creations, featuring animal finials and lush botanical motifs, are represented in the Metropolitan Museum of Art and even the White House, which holds his Empire-style plateau and Bayard family serving dishes.

Colin Van Gelder Forbes and his sons continued the trade into the mid-19th century, producing both plain and richly decorated silver under marks such as "C.V.G.F." and "W. Forbes." William Forbes (1798–1888), the last active silversmith of the line, worked until 1864 before retiring to New Jersey. Across nearly a century, the Forbes silversmiths shaped New York's luxury trade, leaving behind masterpieces that preserve the family's artistry and legacy.

Part V — Achievement

Bishop Alexander Forbes (1564–1617)

Alexander Forbes, born in 1564 to John Forbes of Ardmurdo and Helen Graham of Morphie, descended from a cadet branch of the Forbeses of Little Kildrummy. Educated at St Andrews, he earned an M.A. in 1585 and became minister of Fettercairn in 1588, soon emerging as a significant figure in the Church of Scotland's struggle between Presbyterian and Episcopalian governance. In 1603 he was selected by King James VI to travel to London after Elizabeth I's death and return with royal instructions for maintaining unity within the Kirk.

In 1604 Forbes was appointed Bishop of Caithness, though he continued to serve at Fettercairn. A trusted supporter of the king, he sat in the pivotal 1610 General Assembly, where Episcopacy was formally restored—an event widely criticized for royal pressure and bribery. He was consecrated bishop in 1611 under the new episcopal order and, in 1616, promoted to the Bishopric of Aberdeen, where he was installed in February 1617. He died later that year and was succeeded by his kinsman Patrick Forbes of Corse.

Bishop Patrick Forbes of Corse (1564 – 1635)

Patrick Forbes, 5th Laird of Corse, was born to William Forbes, Laird of Corse and Elizabeth Strachan on August 24, 1564, at Corse Castle. In January 1618, Patrick Forbes succeeded Alexander Forbes as Bishop of Aberdeen. Forbes was appointed Chancellor of King's College of the University of Aberdeen. In that role, he oversaw the repair of many buildings; he increased the library; revived the professorships of divinity, canon law, and physic; and procured the addition of a new professorship in divinity.

Forbes began to suffer from apoplexy and died on March 28, 1635. He was buried in Aberdeen Cathedral.

William Forbes of Menie and Craigievar (1566-1627)

William Forbes of Menie and Craigievar was the younger brother of Bishop Patrick Forbes, who financed William's first attempts at trade. After several failures, William built a substantial fortune trading Baltic timber from the port of Danzig, earning the nickname "Danzig Willie." With his wealth, William acquired the barony of Craigievar from the indebted Mortimer family in 1610. William raised the height of Craigievar Castle and embellished the exterior with bold corbelling and carved stonework. In 1603 he married Margaret Woodward, daughter of the Provost of Edinburgh. When he died in 1627 at age 61, he left not only wealth and estates but a lasting architectural and familial legacy that shaped the future of the Forbes of Craigievar.

Rev. John Forbes of Corse (1568 – 1634)

John Forbes was born around 1568, the son of William Forbes, 4th Laird of Corse, and younger brother of Bishop Patrick Forbes. John studied theology and philosophy at the University of St Andrews and in 1593 became minister of Alford. In 1605, he presided over an unauthorized General Assembly. Refusing the King's order to dissolve, Forbes and several ministers were arrested, tried, and banished in 1606. He settled in the Netherlands, ministering to the Presbyterian community in Middelburg. He founded the English Synod in 1621, serving as its first President. He continued to defend Presbyterianism before both James VI and Charles I. His sons John and Arthur became colonels in the Dutch military service and son James became minister of Abercorn. Forbes died in the Netherlands in 1634.

Bishop William Forbes (1585 – 1634)

William Forbes served the parishes of Alford and then Monymusk in Aberdeenshire. He was admitted as one of the ministers of St. Giles Cathedral in March 1622. In 1633, Forbes preached at Holyrood before Charles I, who was in Scotland for his coronation. The King was so pleased that he created the Scottish Episcopal Diocese of Edinburgh specifically for him. Forbes was consecrated in St. Giles' Cathedral as its first bishop on January 23, 1634. St. Giles Cathedral on the Royal Mile boasts a statue of "Bishop Forbes" on the right-hand side of the west entrance.

Alexander Forbes, 4th Lord Pitsligo (1680 – 1762)

Born in 1678, Alexander Forbes was educated in France, which sparked his lifelong interest in religious philosophy. As the 4th Lord Pitsligo, he entered the Scottish Parliament in 1700 and opposed the Acts of Union. He left Parliament in protest when the Acts passed. In 1715, he joined the Jacobite army under the Earl of Mar and, after defeat at Sheriffmuir, he spent several years abroad before returning quietly to Pitsligo Castle.

When Bonnie Prince Charlie renewed Jacobite hopes in 1745, Pitsligo—then in his late sixties—again took the field. He raised a troop of horse, received a commission as colonel, and served with distinction. After the Jacobite defeat at the 1746 Battle of Culloden, he was attainted, his property seized, and outlawed but evaded capture for 16 years.

Duncan Forbes, 5th Laird of Culloden (1685 – 1747)

Duncan Forbes of Culloden was born at Bunchrew House in 1685. In 1715, he and his elder brother John raised companies who defended Inverness from a Jacobite siege. He inherited the Culloden estate when his brother died in 1734. He served in Parliament before becoming Lord President of the Court of Session, Scotland's highest judicial office. During the 1745 rebellion, he raised troops in the Highlands and convinced many clan chiefs from joining Charles Edward Stuart. Culloden House was commandeered by Stuart prior to the 1746 Battle of Culloden. After the Jacobite defeat, Forbes opposed excessive reprisals. Financially ruined by the war and unreimbursed expenses, he died in 1747. A statue of him was erected in the Old Parliament House, Edinburgh, in 1752.

Brig. General John Forbes (1707 – 1759)

John Forbes was born at Pittencrief House in 1707 and received his commission as captain in the British army in 1744. He rose to Lieutenant-Colonel of the Scots Greys in 1750 and fought for the British government at the 1746 Battle of Culloden, where the Jacobites were defeated. In 1757, Forbes was promoted to Brigadier General and given command of an attack on the French stronghold Fort Duquesne in Pennsylvania. Among his command was the militia led by 26-year-old Colonel George Washington. He secured Fort Duquesne and ordered the construction of Fort Pitt, named after British Secretary of State Pitt the Elder. He also established a settlement that became the site of modern Pittsburgh. He returned to Philadelphia, where he died in 1759.

Bishop Robert Forbes (1708 –1775).

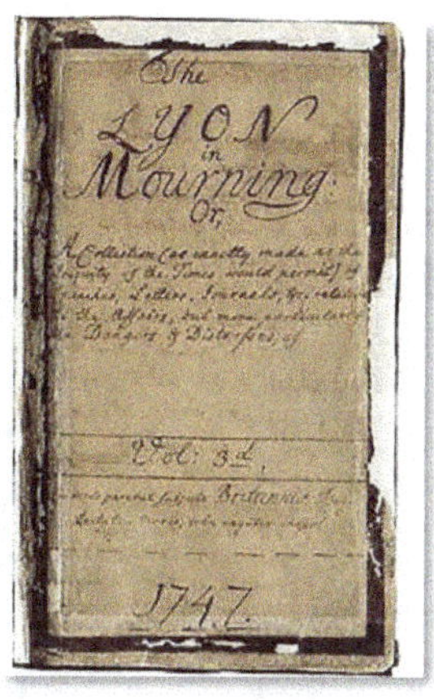

In 1745, Rev. Robert Forbes attempted to join the Jacobite army raised by Charles Edward Stuart. However, he was arrested and imprisoned for the entire coup attempt. Stuart's defeat did not daunt Forbes's zeal for the Jacobite cause. In 1747, he began collecting materials that would eventually become the ten volumes of what he called *The Lyon in Mourning, or A Collection of Speeches Letters Journals Etc. Relative To the Affairs of Prince Charles Edward Stuart*. In 1762, Rev. Forbes was appointed Scottish Episcopal Bishop of Ross and Caithness. He died in 1775. *The Lyon in Mourning* changed hands several times until 1871, when it was presented to the Advocates Library, which became the National Library of Scotland.

Admiral John Forbes (1714 – 1796).

John Forbes was the second son of George Forbes, 3rd Earl of Granard in Ireland. He joined the Royal Navy at the age of 12 in 1726. He was promoted to captain in 1737 and given the command of five battle ships. Forbes was promoted to Rear-Admiral in 1747. In 1755, Forbes was promoted to Vice-Admiral and in 1756 he was appointed a Lord Commissioner of the Admiralty on the Board of Admiralty. Forbes went on to serve as a Lord Commissioner of the Admiralty under successive Governments and later served as Member of Parliament for St Johnstown, Ireland, and then as Member of Parliament for Mullingar in the Parliament of Ireland. His final promotion was to Admiral of the Fleet in 1781.

John Forbes of Skellater (1733 – 1808)

John "Ian Roy" Forbes, second son of George Forbes, 5th Laird of Skellater, was born around 1733 and earned his nickname from his red hair. Raised in a staunch Jacobite household but was too young to join the 1745 rebellion. Ian Roy later joined the Jacobite exile community in France and quickly distinguished himself in the French army. He fought at Maastricht in 1748, later serving in the Seven Years' War. After a notorious attempted duel with John Wilkes in Paris, he left for Portugal, where his military brilliance led to rapid promotion. He became Field-Marshal, Adjutant-General, and a decorated commander in the War of the Pyrenees. Ian Roy accompanied the Portuguese Royal Family to Brazil in 1807 and died in Rio de Janeiro in 1808, "a virtuous and honourable man with undaunted courage."

Sir William Forbes of Pitsligo 6th Bart. (1739–1806)

Sir William Forbes inherited the baronetcy at age four after the death of his father, leaving him and his mother in modest circumstances. His family had long struggled financially—his great-grandfather lost the Monymusk estates, and his Pitsligo relatives were ruined after supporting the Jacobite risings. He was apprenticed with the Edinburgh banking firm of Coutts. Starting in 1754, Forbes rose from apprentice to clerk to partner, eventually leading the respected house of Forbes, Hunter & Co. The firm later became part of the Union Bank of Scotland. Sir William regained the Pitsligo estates in 1781. A generous civic leader, he supported schools, hospitals, and charitable institutions across Edinburgh. He died in 1806.

John "Bombay Jock" Forbes (1743 – 1821)

John was born to John Forbes, 2nd Laird of Bellabeg, and Christian Shepherd, daughter of Rev. John Shepherd of Logie Coldstone. He joined the East India Company in 1764. In 1767, he created Forbes & Company, Ltd., to conduct the business of trading Indian cotton. As the Indian trade with Great Britain boomed, Forbes diversified into shipping, shipbuilding, and banking. His bank business developed into the State Bank of India. John Forbes returned to Britain in 1796 where he acquired his nickname "Bombay Jock." He purchased many Forbes ancestral lands, including the estates of Newe. "Bombay Jock" was also involved in many charitable endeavors. When Forbes died in 1821, he left his estates of Newe to his nephew Charles Forbes, who had taken on the Forbes business in India.

Anne Forbes (1745 – 1834)

When Anne Forbes was 15, her father Hugh died in 1760. In 1767, family friend Robert Chalmers encouraged her to study art in Italy and arranged for financial support of £200 pounds per year for three years. In Rome, she studied under Scottish artists Gavin Hamilton and James Nevay. Forbes moved to Edinburgh in 1772 to "make a comfortable living" from painting and teaching. In 1788 she was appointed Portrait Painter to the Society of Antiquaries in Edinburgh.

James Forbes (1749 – 1819)

James Forbes became a writer for the British East India Company and in 1765 travelled to India where he lived until 1784. He filled a hundred and fifty folio volumes (fifty-two thousand pages) of manuscript pages with detailed notes and sketches on all aspects of wildlife and culture.

When he returned to Great Britain in 1784, Forbes began editing what he called, *Oriental Memoirs*, "selected and abridged from a series of familiar letters written during seventeen years residence in India: including observations on parts of Africa and South America, and a narrative of occurrences in four India voyages." The four volumes were published between 1813 and 1815. He is honored in name of a town in the state of Bihar, India.

Sir William Forbes of Callendar (1756–1823)

Sir William Forbes of Callendar rose from a distinguished line of Aberdeenshire coppersmiths to become one of the wealthiest landowners in Scotland. A descendant of Sir Alexander Forbes, 2nd Laird of Pitsligo, he represented the third generation of a metalworking family.

He patented cold-rolled copper bolts and secured major government contracts to supply the Royal Navy. His role in sheathing warships in copper earned him the enduring nickname "Copper-bottom

Forbes." Wealth from these contracts enabled him to purchase the long-forfeited Livingston estate of Callendar in 1783, elevating him to the style of Sir William Forbes, 1st of Callendar. When Sir William died in 1823, he left an estate that would become, by 1873, the richest branch of the Forbes family, owning 57,000 acres.

Sir Charles Forbes of Newe and Edinglassie, 1st Baronet (1774 – 1849)

Born in 1774 to the Rev. George Forbes of Leochel and Katherine Stewart, Charles Forbes was a great-grandson of George Forbes of Bellabeg and a direct descendant of the Forbeses of Newe and of Lord Pitsligo. At sixteen, Charles left Aberdeen University to join his uncle John Forbes in Bombay. John had founded Forbes & Company in 1767, a mercantile firm that grew into a major force in shipping, banking, and cotton trading. Under their leadership, the company became banker to  the Government of Bombay and regained the long-lost Forbes estates of Newe and Bellabeg.

Returning to Scotland around 1810, Charles married Elizabeth Cotgrave and entered politics. He served in Parliament from 1812 to 1832, representing Beverley and later Malmesbury. He fiercely opposed the Reform Act of 1832—yet, in debate, made a striking argument for women's suffrage by noting that women already voted for East India Company directors. A devoted advocate for India, Forbes championed public works, including securing funds for clean water in Bengal. Honored with a baronetcy in 1823, he died in 1849. His legacy endures not only through the Forbes estates but also through Forbes & Company, one of the world's oldest surviving businesses. In 1823, he founded the Lonach Highland and Friendly Society, which produces the annual Lonach Highland Gathering and Games.

Sir John Forbes MD (1787 – 1861)

John Forbes served in the Royal Navy as a surgeon between 1807 and 1816. After his discharge, Forbes translated the work of René Laënnec who had invented the stethoscope. This greatly expanded the use of the stethoscope among British doctors. Forbes conducted his own innovative medical work regarding the use of the stethoscope in 1824. Forbes was elected a Fellow of the Royal Society in 1829. In collaboration with Dr John Conolly and Alexander Tweedie, Forbes launched a *Cyclopaedia of Practical Medicine* in four volumes (Forbes et al. 1832-35). In 1836, Forbes and Conolly started the *British and Foreign Medical Review, or, A Quarterly Journal of Practical Medicine.* In 1841, Forbes was appointed court physician to Prince Albert and the royal household – a post that he held until his death in 1861.

Captain Robert Bennet Forbes (1804 – 1889)

In 1817, Robert Bennet Forbes left his home in Boston to join the crew of the *Canton Packet,* owned by his uncle Thomas Perkins. He became a full captain in 1825 for the family business, Perkins & Company, which included trade in opium. The company merged with Russell & Company in 1830. In 1847, he and his brother John Murray Forbes shipped food in the *USS Jamestown* to Ireland during the "Great Famine." Captain Forbes detailed his mission in a report to the Committee called "The Voyage of the Jamestown on Her Errand of Mercy." This was the first international relief effort conducted by the United States. His family home in Milton is now the Forbes House Museum.

Edward Forbes (1815–1854)

Edward Forbes, FRS, FGS, was born on the Isle of Man in 1815 into a Forbes family long rooted in Corvalla and Bellabeg. He studied art in London and medicine at Edinburgh but soon devoted himself entirely to natural history. Between 1833 and 1838, he traveled widely across Europe and North Africa, publishing influential studies on botany, zoology, and geology. His 1838 work *Malacologia Monensis* catalogued Manx mollusks. Forbes became curator of the Geological Society's museum

(1842), professor of botany at King's College London (1843), and paleontologist to the Geological Survey (1844).

Katherine Mary Furbish (1834 – 1931)

A descendant of a Scottish prisoner of war from the 1650 Battle of Dunbar, Katherine (Kate) Mary Furbish developed a love for the outdoors and the plants of the state of Maine. She studied art and botany in Paris and Boston.

In 1880, Forbes discovered a new variety of lousewort which botanists named the Furbish lousewort. Her voluminous notes and drawings of plants have been included in institutions such as Harvard University and Bowdoin College in her hometown of

Brunswick, Maine. She was actively engaged in many botany societies. An elementary school and a nature preserve were named in her honor in Brunswick.

Archibald Forbes (1838 – 1900)

Born in Morayshire in 1838, Archibald Forbes was the son of Rev. Lewis William Forbes, Moderator of the Church of Scotland. After leaving Aberdeen University in debt, he enlisted in the 1st Royal Dragoons, where he began writing for major newspapers. In 1870 Forbes became a correspondent for the *Daily News*. His vivid, high-risk reporting helped define the modern war correspondent. He went on to cover conflicts in Spain, Serbia, Turkey, Afghanistan, and Zululand. Celebrated worldwide, he lectured extensively—introduced once by Mark Twain—and continued writing until his death in 1900. He is buried in Aberdeen's Allenvale Cemetery, with a memorial in St. Paul's Cathedral, London.

Edwin Austin Forbes (1839 – 1895)

Edwin Austin Forbes began studying at the National Academy of Design in New York City at the age of 18. In 1861, *Frank Leslie's Illustrated Newspaper* hired Forbes as an artist and deployed him with the Union Army during the American Civil War. Forbes sketched both major battles and daily camp life in the Union army. These sketches formed the basis of his book *Life Studies of the Great Army* in 1876. At the 1876 Centennial Exposition, he was awarded a medal for this book. In 1877, he was made an honorary member of the London Etching Club. In 1890, he completed a 2-volume work called *Thirty Years After: An Artist's Story of the Great War*. His work can now be found in the U.S. National Archives and the Library of Congress.

Sara Forbes Bonetta (1843 – 1880)

In 1847, Frederick Edwyn Forbes was given the command of *HMS Bonetta*. In 1849, Queen Victoria sent Commander Forbes on a mission to the African nation of Dahomey to negotiate peace among the tribes. When he arrived in 1850, he saw a small slave girl, names Omoba Aina, who was to be put to death. He convinced the Dahoman King to spare her life. Forbes brought the girl to Freetown, Sierra Leone, where she was baptized as Sarah Forbes Bonetta. Forbes brought Bonetta to Great Britain and introduced her to Queen Victoria, who made Bonetta her goddaughter and became responsible for Sarah's finances and education.

Stanhope Alexander Forbes (1857 – 1947)

Born in Dublin to William and Juliette Forbes, Stanhope Alexander Forbes showed early artistic promise and trained in London, Brussels, and Paris, where he developed his lifelong interest in painting outdoor scenes and everyday rural life. In 1884 he travelled to Newlyn, Cornwall, intending a brief stay but instead finding the landscape and artistic community deeply inspiring. There he met Canadian artist Elizabeth Armstrong. The two married in 1889 and became central figures in the Newlyn artists' colony. Stanhope's celebrated painting "The Health of the Bride" (1889) established his reputation for sympathetic, narrative realism. In 1899, Stanhope and Elizabeth founded the Forbes School of Painting, which shaped generations of artists. After Elizabeth's death in 1912, Stanhope continued to paint and teach until closing the school in 1938. He died in Newlyn in 1947 at age 89.

George William Forbes (1869 – 1947)

George William Forbes was born in Lyttelton, New Zealand, to sailmaker Robert Forbes. In 1908, He was elected to the New Zealand House of Representatives. In 1927, Forbes became one of two deputy leaders. In 1930, Forbes became Prime Minister and held office for five years during the Great Depression. In 1935, Forbes was awarded the King George V Silver Jubilee Medal and in 1937, he was awarded the King George VI Coronation Medal. Forbes retained his parliamentary seat until 1943, when he retired after 35  years as a Member of Parliament. The George Forbes Memorial Library was established at Lincoln University near Christchurch, New Zealand.

B.C. Forbes (1880 – 1954)

At the age of 14, Bertie Charles (B.C.) Forbes became an apprentice for the *Dundee Courier* in Scotland. In 1901, he went to South Africa to cover the Boer War and in 1902 started the *Rand Daily Mail* in Johannesburg. In 1904, he worked for the *Journal of Commerce* in New York City. In 1917, B.C. became an American citizen and published his first book *Men Who are Making America*. He and Walter Drey started a bimonthly magazine originally planned to be called *Doers and Doings* but eventually called simply *Forbes*. The  magazine dominated business journalism by blending hard financial reporting with personality-driven lists and rankings. B.C. remained editor-in-chief until his death of a heart attack in New York City in 1954. The Forbes media empire is now reputed to be worth about $400 million.

Beatrice Forbes-Robertson Hale (1883 – 1967)

Beatrice Forbes-Robertson was born in England and became a professional actress at the age of 17. In 1907, Forbes-Robertson moved to New York City and joined the New Theatre Company. She was also an outspoken advocate for a woman's right to vote and was an active lecturer. In 1914, she wrote the book *What Women Want: An Interpretation of the Feminist Movement.* During World War I, she was president of the British War Relief Association and raised funds in New York for military hospitals abroad.

Esther Louise Forbes (1891 – 1967)

Esther Louise Forbes was born as the youngest of five children in Westborough, Massachusetts. In 1915, she won the O. Henry Prize for short fiction in the United States. In 1919, she joined the Houghton Mifflin Company in Boston. From 1924 to 1926, she wrote feature articles for the *Boston Evening Transcript.* In 1926, Forbes published her first novel, *O Genteel Lady!,* which was selected by the Book of the Month Club. Forbes wrote *Paul Revere and the World He Lived In,* which won the 1943 Pulitzer Prize in History. She followed this

with the juvenile fiction *Johnny Tremain.* In 1944, the book won the Newberry Award for children's literature. In 1949, she was elected a Fellow of the American Academy of Arts and Sciences. In 1960, Forbes became the first woman elected to membership in the American Antiquarian Society.

Dame Katherine Jane Trefusis Forbes, DBE (1899 – 1971)

Katherine Jane Trefusis Forbes was born in Taltal, Antofagasta, Chile, the youngest daughter of civil engineer Edmund Batten Forbes. In 1916, at the height of World War I, she left school and volunteered for the Women's Volunteer Reserve. She later received her commission as a second Lieutenant. In 1936, Forbes assisted in launching the Emergency Service. Forbes was appointed Chief Instructor of the Auxiliary Territorial Service School of Instruction in 1938. Three months before the beginning of World War II, she was appointed as Director of the Women's Auxiliary Air Force. In January 1944, Forbes was appointed a Dame Commander of the Order of the British Empire (DBE).

Athol Stanhope Forbes (1912 – 1981)

In 1935, Athol Stanhope Forbes entered the Royal Air Force (RAF.) In 1940, Forbes was posted to No. 6 Operational Training Unit (OTU) for a fighter conversion course. He was then appointed flight commander for Squadron 303, a joint venture with the Polish Government in Exile. Forbes was credited with destroying over seven enemy aircraft and sharing credit for two. In 1940, Forbes was awarded two Distinguished Flying Crosses (D.F.C.) In July 1943, he was promoted to Wing Commander. In 1942, Forbes and Squadron Leader Hubert Allen, DFC, compiled the book *Ten Fighter Boys* which included the stories of the pilots of Squadron 303. In 1944, Forbes was awarded an Officer of the British Empire (OBE.) He left the RAF in 1948.

Nigel Ivan, 22nd Lord Forbes (1918 – 2013)

Nigel Ivan Forbes, born 19 February 1918, was the eldest son of Atholl Laurence, 21st Lord Forbes, and Lady Mabel Anson. Educated at Harrow and Sandhurst, he was commissioned into the Grenadier Guards in 1938. During the retreat to Dunkirk in 1940, he was wounded yet he returned to serve in North Africa, Sicily, and France. He later joined the staff of the 5th Guards Armoured Brigade. In 1942 he married the Hon. Rosemary Hamilton-Russell. After the war, he served in Palestine before taking over the Forbes Estate in 1947. He founded the Harthill Farms Partnership and established his family home at Balforbes. Forbes entered national politics as a Scottish Representative Peer in 1955. He served as Minister of State for Scotland (1958–59), promoting agriculture, tourism, and technical education. In 1960 he was awarded a Knight of the British Empire (KBE). A director of Grampian Television and numerous civic organizations, he supported Clan Forbes abroad and led wildlife safaris in East Africa. Remembered as "a pillar of Aberdeenshire life," he died on March 5, 2013.

Bart Forbes (born 1939)

Bart Forbes is one of the most influential American illustrators of the past half-century, celebrated for a career that bridges commercial art, sports imagery, and fine-art painting. Born in 1939 in Altus, Oklahoma, he grew up in an Air Force family whose frequent relocations exposed him to varied landscapes and cultures. Forbes earned a BFA from the University of North Carolina in 1961, served briefly in the U.S. Army, and continued his training at the ArtCenter College of Design in Los Angeles.

In 1967, Forbes moved to Dallas—then an emerging hub for commercial art—where he built a national career. His illustrations appeared in *Time, Sports Illustrated, Ladies' Home Journal, McCall's,* and *Golf Digest,* and he later completed major commissions for NBC, ABC, the NFL, Pepsi, Exxon, and General Electric. Forbes also designed more than twenty U.S. postage stamps and served as Official Artist for the 1988 Seoul Olympics, later contributing art for the 1992 and 1996 Games. Honored as Sports Artist of the Year in 1986 and inducted into the Society of Illustrators Hall of Fame in 2017, Forbes is represented in the Smithsonian, presidential libraries, the Olympic Museum in Seoul, and major private collections.

Kate Elizabeth Forbes (born 1990)

Born on April 6, 1990, in Dingwall, Kate Elizabeth Forbes spent part of her childhood in India, where her father worked with mission hospitals. She later attended a Gaelic school, earned a BA in history from Cambridge, and completed an MSc in migration history at the University of Edinburgh.

Forbes worked for the Scottish Parliament, Oxfam Scotland, and as a chartered accountant with Barclays. She was elected as an Member of Scottish Parliament (MSP) for Skye, Lochaber and Badenoch in 2016. In 2018 she became Minister for Public Finance and Digital Economy, and in 2020 she was appointed Cabinet Secretary for Finance, later expanding her portfolio to the economy. Forbes married Alasdair MacLennan in 2021 and welcomed a daughter in 2022. She ran for SNP leadership in 2023, finishing second. In 2024, First Minister John Swinney appointed her Deputy First Minister of Scotland.

Part VI — Clan Forbes Society

History and Mission

Clan Forbes Society, Inc., is a charitable, cultural and educational organization dedicated to promoting the heritage and legacy of the Scottish House of Forbes. A surname or genealogical connection is not required to join. The current Society incorporated in 2018 continues the work of an early

society that had become dormant ten years previously. As stated by Clan Chief, Malcolm, Lord Forbes, "there is every reason for encouragement to be given to anyone who would like to be associated with our peaceful clan, where grace is our guide."

Programs and Initiatives

The Clan Forbes Society offers a wide range of programs designed to deepen members' understanding of Forbes history and strengthen community ties. Its initiatives include educational articles, heritage resources, and a growing digital archive featuring clan history, biographies, and cultural materials. The Society is a regular sponsor of the Lonach Highland Gathering and Games in Strathdon,

Aberdeenshire. The Society is also dedicated to restoration of heritage sites, such as the Keig Old Kirk, the final resting place for five past clan chiefs. Regular communication, including newsletters, blogs, and videoconferences keep members connected.

The Clan Forbes Society has also organized and hosted heritage tours, which offer members a journey through the heart of Forbes country.

Participants begin in Old Aberdeen, walking medieval streets and viewing rare Forbes manuscripts and artifacts. Participants are welcomed for private, exclusive tours of Druminnor Castle, the earliest Forbes stronghold, and Castle Forbes, home of clan chief Malcolm, Lord Forbes. Travelers also visit a remarkable series of Forbes castles, such as Pitsligo, Tolquhon, Corse, Craigievar, and Pitsligo. The tour culminates with the Lonach Highland Gathering and Games.

Membership

Individuals may join as Affiliate Members and receive free monthly email newsletters. For annual fee of $25 or a one-time fee of $600, Active and Patron Members receive a certificate, access to the private archives, invitation to online clan gatherings with other members and their clan chief, and discounts from  partner Scottish vendors and publications. Participation includes engaging in educational resources, attending events, contributing to community initiatives, and supporting the Society's mission to preserve and share Forbes heritage. Visit www.Clan-Forbes.org to learn more.

B.R. Forbes is a historian and storyteller who illuminates Scotland's rich, intricate past and the people who shaped it.

Forbes revitalized the Clan Forbes Society, incorporating the current organization after the original had gone dormant. As the Society's primary content creator, he built a digital presence that includes an extensive website, Instagram and Facebook accounts, and a growing category of videos on the Society's YouTube Channel. He has led Forbes Heritage Tours in Scotland in 2022, 2024, and 2026, and maintains active relationships with key clan figures, including Clan Chief Malcolm, Lord Forbes of Castle Forbes, and Alexander D. Forbes of Druminnor Castle.

Recognized as the foremost authority on the global House of Forbes, his work draws deeply from primary documents, historical manuscripts, and a broad literary tradition. His scholarship reveals the human drama behind political alliances, clan rivalries, and the religious and cultural upheavals that shaped early modern Scotland.

He resides in Texas with his husband, Antonio Uribe, Jr.

Did you enjoy this book?

★ ★ ★ ★ ★

Reviews let other readers know how this book made a

difference and help authors reach new audiences.

Please take a moment to post a review

on your favorite retailer's site.

Your feedback matters more than you know.

Thank you!

 @ClanForbesSociety

Interested in joining the Clan Forbes Society?

Visit www.Clan-Forbes.org by scanning the QR code below.